CW01497697

CHARLES
1787

HIGH THEORY / LOW CULTURE
Analysing popular television and film

Images
of culture

The series will publish work from the John Logie Baird Centre for Research in Television and Film. The Centre is committed to the analysis and understanding of the history of the institutions of cinema and television and to the analysis of the aesthetic forms which these institutions have produced. While drawing on contemporary critical theory and its development of semiotics, psychoanalysis, and Marxism, the work of the Centre is committed to specific analyses and to a dialogue with practitioners. A commitment to a positive discrimination within popular culture and to an engagement with the politics of the media will be a feature of work in this series.

also in this series

THE BBC AND PUBLIC SERVICE BROADCASTING

COLIN MACCABE *editor*

HIGH THEORY / LOW CULTURE
Analysing popular television and film

MANCHESTER
UNIVERSITY PRESS

Published by MANCHESTER UNIVERSITY PRESS,
Oxford Road, Manchester, M13 9PL, UK

BRITISH LIBRARY CATALOGUING IN PUBLICATION DATA
High theory/low culture: analysing popular television and film. — (Images of culture) 1. Moving-pictures — Social aspects 2. Television broadcasting — Social aspects
1. MacCabe, Colin   II. Series
302.2'34   PN1995.9.S6

ISBN 0 7190 1950 8
ISBN 0 7190 1951 6 *paperback*

TYPESET IN GALLIARD BY KOINONIA LTD, MANCHESTER

Printed in Great Britain
BY THE ALDEN PRESS, OXFORD

Contents

Notes on Contributors

Colin MacCabe is Professor of English at the University of Pittsburgh and Chairman of the John Logie Baird Centre for Research in Television and Film

John Caughie is Lecturer in the Department of Drama, University of Glasgow

Jane Feuer is Assistant Professor in the Department of English, University of Pittsburgh

Simon Frith is Lecturer in the Department of Sociology, University of Warwick

Douglas Gomery teaches at the University of Maryland and lives in Washington, D.C.

Laura Kipnis is a video artist and an Assistant Professor at the University of Michigan

Tania Modleski teaches in the Department of English, University of Wisconsin-Milwaukee

Laura Mulvey is a film maker and film theorist currently teaching at the London College of Printing

Gillian Skirrow is Lecturer in the Department of Film and Television Studies, University of Strathclyde

Andrew Tolson is Lecturer in Communication Studies, Queen Margaret College, Edinburgh

PREFACE

Over the past ten years there has been an ever-increasing interest in the analysis of television. There is now a very respectable bibliography of studies on various aspects of television production. It is, however, relatively uncontroversial to say that much of this research has been doggedly and uninterestingly empirical. The justification of the study of television in both schools and universities is still remarkably defensive and is usually couched in terms of relevance or necessity ('what else can you teach kids?') rather than more positive values. Television seems to pose more clearly than ever various perennial problems in the analysis and study of popular art forms, and in so doing it reflects back on previous analyses of popular forms of film.

Strategies for the analysis of popular culture are remarkable in their general poverty. Polemically one could identify five standard responses:

1   *The intellectual's case*

This, which is the most widespread and successful strategy, re-finds the terms of high culture where you least expect them. The aim is to produce an account of complexity and tradition such that a hitherto despised art from can rival traditional ones. The most spectacularly successful exponents of this strategy were the *Cahiers du Cinéma* critics in the 1950s. It could be argued that the radical aesthetics of the 1970s, which placed sexual difference and its problematisation at the centre of their concerns, can be seen as merely a version of this strategy in which the complexity of the articulation of castration becomes the crucial evaluative nexus.

2 *The proletarian appeal*

This approach lays emphasis on areas of social reality unavailable to high art. The importance of popular art is thus identified in relation to a contemporary or past social reality which is not represented within traditions of high art. Such a position often leads to celebration rather than analysis.

3 *The structuralist turn*

The structuralist solves the division between high and popular culture by dissolving it. Structuralist method refuses to differentiate amongst its objects. All cultural forms are analysed in relation to a series of contradictions and oppositions which are variously realised across all signifying systems.

4 *The aesthete's move*

This embodies a refusal of analysis in favour of an enthusiastic celebration of detail as the foundation for evaluation and comparison. This strategy takes refuge in the fetishism of the incidental. Here popular becomes 'pop'.

5 *The hedonist's fancy*

In this case, all problems with the popular are displaced by concentrating on pleasure. Unfortunately this merely relocates the problems at a different level.

In March 1984 the John Logie Baird Centre for Research in Television and Film organised a seminar on popular culture with a dual aim. On the one hand, to understand the above mentioned strategies better and to ask how far any of them really focused the problem of the definition and evaluation of popular culture and, on the other, to confront, across a series of histories and genres, the particular problems posed by television and film. It was appropriate that the Baird Centre should choose this topic for its first seminar as the Centre's whole *raison d'être* is to try to understand the popularity of television (and, to a lesser degree, film) aesthetically and historically – to grasp the full cultural significance of the combinations of sound and image so dominant in the life of the twentieth century.

The overall success of the seminar is not really for me to judge, but all the participants felt that we had interested ourselves enough to try to interest others through publishing the proceedings. It is, however, misleading to refer to the papers that follow as proceedings. Some papers from the seminar have been omitted from the book through pressure of space and time; some of the essays here included were not delivered at the seminar, and most have been very extensively re-worked from their initial presentation. But there is enough continuity between the two discursive events to discern common themes. It would be idle to assume exact identity of views, or easily summarisable positions, but throughout the seminar and the editing of this book three emphases recurred:

Popular culture/politics. Any attempt to read popular culture politically needs to be acutely dialectical. The political cannot necessarily be understood independently of the forms of popular culture.

Popular culture/gender. To analyse the functioning and history of popular culture is inevitably to engage in the complex functioning and history of gender and sexuality. Our very understanding of notions of masculinity and femininity are heavily dependent on their figuration in the forms and audiences of popular culture.

Popular culture/high culture. Any sustained consideration of popular culture inevitably erodes the distinction between it and 'high culture'. To develop the force and possibility of much of the energy in popular culture, it is essential that it erupt into the areas of pleasure hitherto defined by the cultural forms bequeathed to us by the Renaissance. This may well be an essential component of any post-modernist aesthetic.

The seminar would not have taken place without the

generous support of Scottish Television, the British Film Institute and the Scottish Film Council. I would particularly like to acknowledge a sense of debt to the late Roddy Maclean for his efforts on the Baird Centre's behalf.

The planning for and the editing that resulted from the seminar on popular culture spanned the first two years of the Centre's existence and of my tenure of the post of its Director. I would like to record, for my own sake if no one else's, how worthwhile I have found that time.

Colin MacCabe
Strathclyde University, 1985

Defining popular culture

This book grows out of a widely felt dissatisfaction. The use of psychoanalytic and semiotic concepts in the analysis of film, which proved so fruitful when applied both to classic Hollywood cinema and much European and American avant-garde film has proved much less successful in its attempt to give an account of either the new Hollywood cinema or, more importantly, television. The forms of analysis which proved so powerful were drawn from a Brechtian aesthetic, and particularly those elements of Brecht which stressed art as a practice which could produce knowledge. What was specific to art was the way in which ideological and political knowledge was dependent on the articulations of symbolic acknowledgement of castration. Psychoanalysis was thus added to Brecht to produce an aesthetic of difference.

From within this aesthetic it is possible to account for the failure to deal with so much contemporary art in terms of the failure of that contemporary art. An argument can be produced that texts such as *ET* or *The Sweeney* are so concerned to disavow the reality of sexual difference that it is impossible to do more than dismiss them as stupifying forms designed to retain their audiences in ignorance and inaction.

The problem with such an argument is that is simply reduplicates certain traditional forms of cultural pessimism and denies any effective form of engagement with contemporary culture. From an educational point of view it has the disastrous effect of suggesting that one teach contemporary culture only to denounce it. Educationally, there must be some way of producing procedures for analysing popular forms of television which will interest and inform children, and if these procedures may, at some stage, re-engage with the aesthetic of difference that I sketched above, they cannot possibly start there. This theoretical problem can also be seen from a practical pedagogic angle. Why is it possible to articulate convincingly dilemmas of castration in *Young Mr Lincoln* and *Touch of Evil,* and why does such an attempt become ludicrously or boringly repetitive when applied to other examples? Could the problem be one of register: that within the still confines of the seminar room or weekend school any text can be made to deliver up its sexual meanings, but that in the noisier ambiance of the classroom or the first year lecture theatre, the lecturer suddenly appears perverse as he or she gamely struggles to explicate the dilemmas of castration; the dialectic of having and being suddenly reduced to the pathetic ramblings of a sex-obsessed adult.

For the moment I wish to leave both problems of educational theory and pedagogic practice in order to consider popular culture from a political perspective. The insights thus gained and the contradictions revealed may then provide some of the terms with which we can return to the educational problems. 'Popular culture' as a term has a very definite history, but if one part of that history is clear, the other is marked by division and uncertainty. The meaning of 'culture' appealed to in the term is in polemical disagreement with those traditonal meanings which attempt to limit culture to a specific corpus of elite practices and a definite canon of works. Instead, to use Williams's famous phrase, culture is understood as 'a whole way of life', embracing a wide variety of practices. Suddenly culture can include much more than the approved genres of opera, painting or literature. But while we can be clear about the polemical meaning of culture, 'popular' remains determindly evasive. Anybody who has, for example, looked at the very successful Open University course on popular culture might be surprised to find that there is no definition of popular culture as such. The course takes its notions of popular culture from a series of over-lapping cultural debates on the left, and makes no effort to arrive at a precise definition. The reasons for this are outlined in a lucid article by the course chairman, Tony Bennett, in *Screen Education* no. 34 which argues that it is impossible to classify popular culture. The article summarises, in order to reject, four major definitions. The first is straightforwardly descriptive – it defines popular in terms of television ratings, record sales and other quantifiable indicators. Such a descriptive approach suffers not only because it has no positive content but also because it will frequently include forms of 'high culture'. A second strategy simply defines popular culture in terms of what is left over when one subtracts traditional cultural forms from our current types of entertainment. Bennett finds this approach equally unsatisfactory as, once again, there is no positive definition to link the heterogenous material derived from this procedure. Thirdly, Bennett considers that culturally pessimistic, generally conservative position which defines popular culture in terms of the new mass forms of entertainment generated by capitalist investment. These new forms are opposed to an older popular 'folk' art in which there is no fundamental division between audience and performer and where meanings are democratically produced. By contrast, the 'mass' art of capitalist society addresses a passive audience which simply registers meanings produced elsewhere. The fourth and final position is a culturally optimistic positive definition which preceives this new 'mass' art as enjoying a more active relationship with its audience and aligns this art with the creative impulses of 'the people'. Such impulses are understood as originating within working-class culture and as opposing dominant bourgeois culture. This is a popular culture brimming over with political potential. For Bennett, both pessimistic and optimistic definitions take far too simple notions of 'imposing from above' and 'emerging from below'. Bennett's solution is to adopt a strategy first sketched by Gramsci and elaborated by Stuart Hall and to cease to talk about any definable object at all. Instead, the social is theorised as overlapping terrains of struggle, and then popular culture is simply a way of specifying areas of resistance to dominant ideological forms. No matter how complex the formulations, this approach conceives of the cultural as a unified totality which can always finally, through however many million mediations, be understood in relation to notions of class and class struggle. Strengths this position undoubtedly has, but is reproduces the weakness of the fourth position which, in some sense, it strives to repair. The meanings of texts, whether located as inhering in the texts themselves or in their interpretations, are always finally anchored in a class struggle which is not to be understood in cultural terms. Popular culture simply becomes a way of conducting economic struggle by other means.

The left's interest in popular culture has always had this element in it: that battles lost economically and politically can be turned into cultural victories. What I now want to consider is how one might pursue a radical interest in popular culture without limiting in advance the politics that will ensue from that interest. A first step will take us to the dictionary. Of course, words do not determine meanings; the flicker of signification can be achieved across the most unpromising material, the fugitive intention can always twist a word into new patterns of meaning. At the same time it is always salutary to recall etymology, not as proof but as a reminder of the semantic fields in which one is operating.

Popular is derived from *populus* – the Latin for 'the people' and 'the people' designated in relation to law. The ruling authority was the Senate and people of Rome and it was from this union that law emanated. Its first recorded meaning in English is also related to law: a popular law was a law that affected all the people. Already we can discern that flicker of meaning which makes popular both so elusive and so central: popular, emanating from the people; popular, applied to the people. The second meaning recorded in the Oxford English Dictionary reveals a further element in its centrality as a term for left politics: 'pertaining to, or consisting of the common people as a whole as distinguished from any particular class; constituted or carried on by the people'. Here we find 'the people' transcending class in a way that avoids objectionable ruling class formulations of the nation or the folk. Here we have the plebian as everyman. The appeal of this meaning is inscribed in the history of the European left since the French popular front government of 1936 and is witnessed in the numerous popular fairs held under the auspices of left parties across Europe each summer. It is Gramsci's concepts of the national-popular and the hegemonic which attempt, within the Marxist tradition, to figure the possibilities of this notion of 'the popular'. Gramsci has the immense merit of refusing the class against class positions which debilitated the European left between 1928 and 1935 and still bequeaths a residual cultural prescriptivism which dooms sections of the left to a ghetto of 'correct' cultural productions. Indeed, even in the seventies, Gramsci could serve as a useful antidote to those sectarian positions which effectively limited political potential to the archive or the avant-garde. If we are to deprive ourselves of the sounds of the radio and the music centre, of the images of the video cassette recorder or the television, then we risk making difficult struggles unwinnable, of leaving ourselves in an echo chamber of intellectual repetition. But if the appeal to Gramsci has this immense merit, it also has the familiar drawbacks of any Hegelian or Marxist analysis of culture. The Hegelian moment assumes that we can describe our culture as a totality and the Marxist moment then derives this description from a class analysis. The differentiation of cultural artefacts becomes a simple gauging of their political effects. The Gramscian argument describes a cultural terrain in which the dominated's resistance of the dominant is always in terms of meanings already politically defined.

What we must consider is a more radical relationship between popular culture and politics in which it is the culture which may often provide the terms to re-evaluate the politics. At this point the academic category of 'popular culture' would suddenly turn vicious, redefining the political commitments which had first sought to employ it. We can move the argument forward by considering the two key meanings that can be garnered from the Oxford English Dictionary. The fourth heading records the meaning 'intended or suited to ordinary people', with a further gloss that this may mean adapted to the taste or the means of the ordinary people. This notion of adaptation to the taste of the ordinary people has a long history, with the entries running back to Gabriel Harvey's pleas in 1573 'in philosophical disputation to give popular and plausible themes' down to the Longmans catalogue list of 1872 which introduced a series devoted to popular science. The sixth meaning, by contrast, has 'finding favour with or approved by the people, liked, beloved or admired by the people – favourite, acceptable, pleasing'. It occasions little surprise that when we turn to the 1980 supplement it is these two meanings that have produced a host of new examples – on the one hand an emphasis on something produced for ordinary people, on the other something approved by the people. It is in the switch between the two emphases that we can locate the problematic of popular culture.

If we stress that popular film and television is produced for the people, then we stress the fact of forms of entertainment which are not generated by the audience either as producers in traditional forms of singing and dancing nor yet in the more active affirmation required by the music hall or the theatre. The audience is figured in forms over which it has no control; in the case of television in a form which invade the home. Immediately a series of criticisms begin to voice themselves around notions of passivity, domination and lack of control. Two options now present themselves. A conservative defence of high culture, a paean of praise for the intellectual effort and social practices required for the appreciation of poetry, painting and classical music. Or a progressive defence of the avant-garde, site of a contestation of the social practices embedded in the high cultural tradition, and a commitment to the intellectual effort of that same tradition. The problem with this progressive alternative is that is inevitably entails attitudes and assumptions which are unacceptable to any kind of committed democratic politics. The millions who daily watch television are discounted in their torpor and their sloth, their tastes held to be of no account, artificial creations of an even more total penetration of capitalist relations of production (the Frankfurt School provides the most elaborate statement of such a position). In fact the only politics which is consistent with such an avant-gardist position would be a traditional Leninist one. A certain form of political organisation, the Party, would guarantee the production of an alternative and more authentically popular view of the society, a fulcrum from which one could move the world, Archimedes as revolutionary. Such ideas now seem to me at best outmoded, depending on a reduction of all practices of the political, and at worst lethal, insisting on such a reduction. What should be stressed, I think, is that many of the avant-garde positions of the late sixties and seventies depend, consciously or not, explicitly or not, on such a conception of politics.

What of the alternative? We are confronted with a whole series of cultural productions which find favour, are approved in numbers which simply beggar historical comparison. Are we thus to go all the way with the democratic argument and claim that in these cultural objects, produced and reproduced throughout the Western world, we find the most authentic register of popular desires? The political conclusion of this argument might be that left political parties should immediately consider a politics that would harness this great machinery of desire and, imitating the Roman emperors, give them circuses as well as bread. If we are to take this option, however, we simply subordinate politics to existing cultural forms as the Leninist position subordinates the existing culture to a future politics.

What I hope to have sketched here are the impasses of the two major left positions on popular culture in a way that indicates how even a version as sophisticated as Bennett's does not escape the problem of simply anchoring choices in a politics which would appear unaffected by the cultural forms themselves. All that I have argued to date merely sets out clearly the problems confronting the analyst of popular culture. I wish to end the chapter with some positive comments but they are, of necessity, much more tentative and provisional then what has gone before.

What seems positive to me in the commitment to popular culture is that element which is determined to break with any and all of the formulations which depend on a high/low, elite/mass distinction. These who isolate themselves within the narrow and exclusive traditions of high art, those who glory in the simple popularity of the popular, both effectively ignore the complex way in which traditions and technologies combine to produce audiences. It is in this figuring of different audiences that the political reality of art can be found – the particular way in which an audience is addressed and constituted in relation to the political forms in which it participates. Crucial in this context is the category of the nation for both the traditional forms of high art and the most closely politically controlled mass forms address an audience, which they thereby constitute, as national. Just as a national literature in the vernacular tongue was an essential component in the constitution of the various ruling classes of the nation states of post-Renaissance Europe, so a national broadcasting system is a crucial element in the current political settlement of the capitalist West. Many of the cultural forms with the greatest political potential, be they works within a high cultural tradition like Joyce's *Ulysses* or Rushdie's *Midnight's Children*, or works within more popular forms, like the music of Motown or the Beatles, break this national grid – asserting regional and racial specificities to transnational audiences. What this might suggest is that we should be looking for political groupings along the fault-lines opened up by these cultural products.

A traditional Marxist, in the wearied tones of the politically hard-bitten, might well retort that this is all very suggestive but that unless cultural forms are related to the institutions that exercise political power – they are still institutions of nation states – then they will simply obscure political realities. But here, as so often, one may doubt the 'evidence' of the political efficacity of the nation state. If one looks at the most powerful movements in the West over the past twenty-five years – the women's movement, the anti-nuclear movement, the ecological movement, even the movement for black rights in 'Western' countries from the United States to South Africa – it is doubtful whether these movements find their deepest reality at the national level. It is also the case that it would be difficult to give an account of the history of woman's or black struggles in the past twenty-five years without considering the way in which those struggles have depended on identifications first formulated in cultural terms. It is, of course, the case that the national level cannot be simply ignored. It is in definite demands posed to specific national governments that many concrete political aims have to be realised. However, it is probably wrong to understand the movements that formulate these aims in national terms. It may be added that it is doubtful whether multinational capital is as convinced of the political importance of the nation state as the supposedly hard-bitten Marxist. The crucial necessity for political action is a felt collectivity. It may be that cultural forms indicate to us that politically enabling collectivities are to be located across subcultures, be they national or international. It may be that the opposition between the popular and the national will come to make the radical edge of cultural politics. Much of this may seem speculative. What is less speculative is that the next ten years are going to witness profound mutations in the geopolitics of entertainment. Traditional left positions, whether couched in the pessimistic tones of the Frankfurt School or the more nuanced accents of Gramsci, are simply unable to provide the terms with which to engage seriously with the coming changes. But engage with them we must.

chapter 2 LAURA KIPNIS

'Refunctioning' reconsidered:
towards a left popular culture[1]

I

A few years ago, almost overnight it seemed, nearly every stop sign on the north side of Chicago was transformed, presumably by local women's groups (presumably at night and with stealth), to read STOP RAPE, by the additions of the word RAPE, spray-painted in reflective white paint directly under the word STOP. The signs would remain in this altered state for a short time, until the city sent work crews out to obliterate the word RAPE with red paint, thus terminating the sign's brief career as a tool of feminist agitation and returning it to its prosaic function in traffic control. Sporadically, midnight spray-painting campaigns would renew the ongoing struggle between the city and women's groups for this highly visible site of address with its guaranteed audience – but the city's resources triumphed and there are very few STOP RAPE signs to be found any more. More recently though, this same tactic has been taken up by another movement: currently affixed to a number of stop signs are stickers which read: US INVOLVEMENT IN NICARAGUA or US SLAUGHTER IN CENTRAL AMERICA. These stickers have been printed expressly for stop signs, so their final messages read: STOP US INVOLVEMENT IN NICARAGUA, or STOP US SLAUGHTER IN CENTRAL AMERICA. And so it goes on the left: feminist interpellations effaced and superseded by more pressing interpellations. (Historians of contemporary cultural expression will no doubt want to note the introduction of mechanical reproduction into this particular sub-genre.)

The use the term 'interpellation' here is deliberately to invoke Louis Althusser's contention that the mechanism of all ideology is the interpellation, or hailing, of individuals, as ideological subjects.[2] To cite the example of the bland and ubiquitous stop sign as an instance of ideological interpellation may seem eccentric (its elimination is not on even the most ultra-left programme as far as I know, since even ultra-leftists must fear, as do we all, the dreaded gridlock; however the intrepid free-enterprise anarchists of the Libertarian Party *have* just announced their opposition to the stop sign).[3] But the STOP of the stop sign does literally echo Althusser's own ironic demonstration of the role of 'recognition' in the process of constituting ideological subjects: the policeman who yells 'Hey, you there!', coupled with the individual who cannot fail to recognise herself as the subject of the interpellation and automatically turns around. To *stop* at a stop sign, then, is to recognise oneself as the subject of the intepellation, and to be ('always-already') engaged in an ongoing process of transformation from concrete individual to concrete (legal/juridical, in this case) subject. This example of the stop sign is further apt in that it makes clear the interplay between ideological interpellation and agencies of state repression. As anyone who has even been caught running a stop sign discovers, the entire array of what Althusser calls the Repressive State Apparatus stands ready to enforce this interpellation should one fail to heed it. (And in Chicago it really is the *entire* array: the newspapers were full of reports a few years ago of traffic violators routinely subjected to strip searches by particularly zealous defenders of the peace.)

These acts of appropriating and transforming stop signs can be said to exemplify political contestation precisely at the level of ideological interpellation. Such transformations enact a struggle over, and within, a particular ideological terrain, between a dominant discourse (Althusser regards the legal system, which would include traffic laws, as a part of both the Ideological and the Repressive State Apparatuses) and an oppositional discourse. To view a stop sign as something worth struggling over may seem politically unambitious, but there are two interesting implications here for a theory of a left popular culture. First, that the prior interpellation, the STOP of state power, is mere 'raw material' that derives its meaning only in relation to its articulation within a particular discourse, and in specific relation to the other elements of that discourse. It does not have pre-assigned, essential meaning, and moreover, its meaning cannot be reduced to an expression of class or nation. The second implication, then, is that these raw materials may be appropriated and transformed by oppositional discourses in order to express antagonisms and resistance to dominant discourses – a process of *disarticulation* from a discourse of which the interpellations were formerly a part, and *rearticulation* to a competing or antagonistic discourse.

The anonymously transformed stop signs are offered as the first example of what I will be calling the 'refunctioning' of dominant forms. The term itself derives from Brecht's phrase 'functional transformation' *(Umfunktionierung)*, coined to convey his position that intellectuals and artists should not merely supply the production process, but should also attempt to transform it, along the lines of existing political struggle.[4] Brecht's attempt to set his contemporaries straight on their unwitting complicity with the political forms they aspire to transform, prefigures a largely unheeded contemporary commonplace: that formal innovation, even when 'revolutionary', can always be assimilated and appropriated by the dominant and dominating culture. The artistic practice that would follow from Brecht's notion of 'refunctioning' is also suggested by the phrase *disarticulation-rearticulation* which occurs in an Althusserian context, most prominently in the writing of the Argentinian Marxist, Ernesto

Laclau.[5]

The purpose of this chapter, then, is to outline the structural possibilities offered for an oppositional cultural practice at the present moment: to assess the possibilities given within postmodernism for cultural politics. This is to suggest that any strategy for a cultural-political practice must take its direction from the structure of which it is a moment, and not from ideal paradigms or timeless formulas. It is provisional.

This suggests, secondly, that the possible moment of a political and contestatory *modernism* – the cultural politics of Adorno, Horkheimer and Marcuse, still upheld by Habermas, and implicitly recreated in the journal *Screen* and much of the current formal analysis of political domination as embedded in practices of signification and at the level of the *text* – this modernist moment has come and gone.

II

The term 'mass', either standing alone, or paired with its ally, 'culture', is a term situated in contradiction. It carries sedimented and contrary implications, alluding as it does to that dubious entity 'the people' – a presence coded positively or negatively depending on the politics of the discourse within which this entity is consciously or unconsciously invoked. There can be, variously, the pejorative connotations of 'low' or 'vulgar', or the suggestion of a positive or potentially positive political and social force – a people acting together in solidarity, as in the *levée en masse* of the French revolution.[6] In that this current and contradictory usage became fully abvailable in the mid-nineteenth century with the birth of modern class society emerging from the rapid industrialisation of Western Europe, the term arrives clearly burdened with a weighty historical residue: not only the evocation of the urban proletariat, but then implicitly the latter's conditions of formation – the economic ascendancy of the bourgeoisie and its attendant consolidation of political power. There are two things, then, to say about this: first, that the terms 'mass' and, concomitantly, 'mass culture', have a particular set of meanings and implications within capitalist society that cannot be evaded. (Or rather, the evasion is symptomatically ahistorical and itself constitutive of a particularly conservative political position *vis à vis* culture.) Secondly, arguments, positions and theories about mass *culture* are coded ways of talking about class.

The latter point makes available a new reading of the last ten years' flurry of theoretical interest and investment in popular culture which goes like this. The present heyday of mass culture studies, it may be noted, occupies the same theoretical moment as what is commonly referred to as the 'crisis in Marxism' or the 'crisis on the left'. This conjunction, given an historically mediated reading of the term 'mass', exposes two historical moments as, roughly, mirror images. In the first is the emergence of the urban proletariat, the seeds of the working class movement and socialist theory – all the previously cited sedimentation of 'mass', which marked the opening of a determinate political space. In the second, that is the present moment, in which post-Marxism has eclipsed and displaced the working class as the 'privileged subject' of history – no longer is it the anticipated agent of social transformation – we find here the emergence of mass *culture* as the 'privileged subject' of left academia: a phantom politics which marks the closing down of that earlier set of political possibilities and marks the loss of what might be called the political subject.

To propose this reading denies theory an autonomous role (as in Althusser), and posits critical discourse as not only a site of production of cultural meanings, but *itself* a product of the conditions it theorises. The current serious attention given to popular culture, which marks a major shift from a time when mass culture was either not worth discussing, or only worth denouncing (two faces of the same consciousness) is here understood then as a product of transformations outside theory.

Whether it was mass cultural forms or contents being indicted, whether it was 'kitsch' or 'debased means-ends rationality' being dismissed, the practices of popular culture were incapable of being adequately theorised in the moderist era. Invoking modernism's relation to the popular and placing that relationship in the unspecified past sets up perhaps a somewhat new periodisation. The current approachability of the popular – the inundation of scholarly books on the subject (this one, for example), the plethora of conferences and journals, a rewritten canon within universities *and* the focus on popular forms on the left – this burgeoning approachability is characteristic of *postmodernism*. (And would also indicate a certain *urgency* to theorisation in this historical configuration.)

If it is held that there is an interpenetration of theory and the object it theorises, then transformations in the object itself (in this case, the field of culture) are what make possible transformations in our knowledge of that object. Peter Burger's *Theory of the Avant-Garde* offers a corollary to this: he argues there that only 'the full unfolding of the constituent elements in a field' makes possible 'an adequate cognition of that field'.[7] An example would be Marx's writing of *Capital*: it takes the full emergence of the urban proletariat, the universal commodification of labour, the reduction of difference to the common denominator of exchange value, etc., before capitalism as a phenomenon can be fully comprehended. A corollary to *this* idea is that these new theoretical developments always bring with them a reinterpretation of history: the conditions that allowed the theorisation of capital simultaneously allowed pre-capitalist economic formations to be construed. Precursors of present developments are discovered in retrospect. This, then, would account for the current spate of re-theorisations of modernism (Burger's book being one) – this is part of the emergence of postmodernism.

An onslaught of theorisation works perhaps like a symptom: its etiology can be uncovered by working backwards from its given components to discover its presuppositions. Freud writes: 'The task is. . . simply to discover, in respect to a useless idea and a pointless action, the past situation in which the idea was justified and the action served a purpose'. One possible presupposition of intensified theorisation about popular culture has been suggested: the shift from a refusal to an embrace of the popular in theoretical discourse marks a break between modernism and postmodernism. We might then surmise that the 'purpose' of the 'symptom' is to be found in the paradigm of *transition* – the indeterminate space opened by such a break – and the compensatory structures this puts into play.

Evidence for a link between theorisation and transition is provided in Michael Taussig's recent *The Devil and Commodity Fetishism in South America*.[8] Based on Taussig's fieldwork, this book details the appearance of a particular set of mythic beliefs, or theorisations, which have arisen 'at a particularly crucial and sensitive point of time in historical development' in distinct areas of rural South America. Regions of both Colombia and Bolivia are undergoing the transformation from what is often referred to as 'traditional society' to 'modern' or 'industrial society' – in other words, from peasant-cultivator, use-value based societies to societies comprised of landless wage-labourers and based on exchange-value. Local peasants have become proletarianised, often through violence and appropriation of land; they are driven to seek employment for wages in the sugar plantations of Colombia and tin mines of Bolivia.

An explanatory mythology has arisen independently in both these societies. It is based on the figure of the devil, who is invoked 'as part of the process of maintaining or increasing production'. In Colombia, certain workers, it is believed, have entered into secret pacts with the devil to increase their production and earn more money. These contracts though, are said to ultimately destroy those who enter into them, for the devil's money is barren: if spent on such capital goods as land or livestock the land willl become sterile and the animals will sicken and die. In Bolivia, Indians create workgroup rituals to the devil who they believe to be the true owner of the tin mines. Rituals like these are meant to sustain production, uncover ore-sources and reduce accidents.

Although the devil is assigned the central role in sustaining production, he is seen at the same time as a 'gluttonous spirit bent on destruction and death'. In both Bolivia and Colombia, while the devil is held to be the mainstay of production or of increasing production, this production is believed to be ultimately destructive of life. (And note that, where the mysterious workings of capital are concerned, how similar is the content of these myths and the quasi-populist anti-big-business sentiments that permeate our own mass culture: our ambivalent fascination with such devilish figures as the tycoon, the power-broker, or J. R. Ewing, the oil baron.)

Late capitalism is not, as some like to say, a post-industrial society, but rather is marked by the complete industrialisation of all segments of society:[9] this we can see currently demonstrated in the increasing mechanisation of the service sector, not to mention the growth of something called the 'leisure' industry, or even telephone sex. In late capitalism, culture as well is subject to the increasing penetration of capital and increasing mechanisation. So we can see that even the most 'advanced' economic system is composed of a discontinuous series of structures, some of which lag far behind others, as these structures evolve at different rates and are asynchronous. Thus, elements of older modes of production co-exist with anticipations of future modes of production, with the result that different areas in any society, are, at any given moment, at quite different stages of development.

This model suggests that observations or theories about one sphere of one social formation at a particular developmental stage might aptly be applied to a *different* sphere of a *second* social formation at a comparable stage of development. For example, Ernesto Laclau, in discussing ways of theorising populism in Latin America – often associated with the transition from a traditional to industrial society – writes about certain basic changes associated with that transition, some of which have obvious resonances with the sphere of culture in *this* society: a 'passage from an institutionalisation of tradition to that of change'; and the 'evolution from a relatively undifferentiated complex of institutions to an increasing differentiation and specialisation of them'.[10] In other words, then, perhaps a structurally similar relationship might also exist between an outbreak of *theory* and social transformation in two dissimilar social formations. Tuassig's fieldwork on the dynamic mediation of oppositions found in devil beliefs in South America – a set of practices seemingly quite distant from popular culture studies – can offer a paradigm for understanding current theorising on popular culture as, in Taussig's words, the mediation 'between two radically distinct ways of apprehending or evaluating the world of persons and things'.

Like Michael Taussig, I am concerned with tracing a transition between two points: that of use-value and that of exchange-value; a transition of industrialisation and capital penetration. The transition outlined here, however, is in this social formation, and specifically in the sphere of culture: it occupies an historical axis running roughly from the point where Walter Benjamin marks the erosion of 'aura' in painting as a correlate of proliferating photographic technology, to a current point, postmodernism, which can be defined, following Guy Debord, as the complete commodification of the image sphere.[11]

Debord's argument cites the 'spectacle' as the commodified form of the image. Like the commodity, it disguises what it really is – relationships among people and classes – into an appearance of the objective and the natural. The spectacle is the capitalist colonisation and monopolisation of the image – it subjugates people to its monopoly of appearance, and proclaims: 'That which appears is good, that which is good appears'.

So while for Althusser, the nature of ideology is, following Jacques Lacan, *specular*, mirror-like: the interpellated subjects recognise themselves in a mirror-like relationship with dominant ideology, for Debord ideology is *spectacular*: the spectacle is 'the existing order's uninterrupted discourse about itself, its laudatory monologue'. The privileged ideological form though, is in both cases, the *representation*.

III

It is only the fact that spectacle has now become the universal category of society as a whole that allows us Debord's understanding of it, Debord writes, echoing Lukács, the theoretician of totality. The cultural transformation that this signifies, which can be abbreviated by the term 'postmodernism', has as its decisive feature the crossing of the previously uncrossable chasm between high and mass culture. This traversal is evidenced by the current embrace of the popular in the production of both 'high culture' and 'high theory'. Both cases significantly depart from the treatment of popular culture in the period of modernism.

Introducing content from mass culture into high art has been an art world convention at least since pop art, which might be said to have terminated modernist cultural hegemony. The strategy has persevered and an influential body of work has recently been produced by a loosely affiliated group of artists (many first associated with a New York gallery called Metro Pictures) which aims to occupy the contemporary intersections of high art and the media. Some of the better-known artists in this group are Dara Birnbaum, who re-edits popular television shows like *Wonder Woman* or *Laverne and Shirley* into art videotapes which are often called 'deconstructions of television' or 'analyses of television codes'; Cindy Sherman, who, with elaborately costumed verisimilitude, transforms herself into a variety of stereotypical female personae, which she then captures in large photographic self-portraits that read like film stills of Hollywood movies; David Salle, whose paintings combine the visual clichés of popular culture and the 'painterly' conventions of high art; and Sherrie Levine, who re-photographs and exhibits the photographs of previous photographic 'greats' like Edward Weston and Walker Evans, signifying a refusal to disseminate new images and a rejection of the conventions and proprieties of authorship.

As I have said, contemporary developments like these never arrive unescorted, but are accompanied by a rewritten history. Postmodernism not only allows, but dictates, a deconstruction of the binarism upon which modernism was enacted, in that postmodernist art *and* theory both foreground a reworking of the false problem of value that programmed the high culture/mass culture split, in which either was read as the absence of the other.

In the binary opposition between high culture and mass culture, as with all binarisms, ideology is at work. The increasing interpenetration of high culture and mass culture that is the 'dominant episteme' of the postmodern, registers the loss of the ideological function of this binarism, both institutionally and within individual cultural texts. Dismantling the ideological scaffold of modernism allows the rereading of modernism as constituted solely within this split, and existing only so long as it could keep its Other – the popular, the low, the regional and the impure – at bay. We could redefine modernism as the ideological necessity of erecting and maintaining exclusive standards of the literary and artistic against the constant threat of incursion or contamination. The partial success of this project is what is generally given to us as the unity, modernism. What did not conform was excluded from consideration. Without the high/low binarism in place, a displacement that can be staged only after the emergence of the postmodern, it is unclear whether modernism as such ever existed at all. (And the ongoing project of feminist art history to provide an alternative account of the period should be mentioned here.)

The narrative of transgression and suppression, rebellion and restoration that emerges from reading the adventures of the high/low culture dialectic against the dialectic of social classes suggests that the 'political unconscious' lurking beneath the patina of culture might be in some way related to the larger ongoing drama of struggles between social groups engendered by class society. At roughly the exact moment at which we can mark the emergence of the 'modern' in the visual arts, the *Salon des Refusés* of 1863, where Manet showed his *Olympia*, a contemporary prostitute painted in the pose of Titian's *Venus of Urbino* – at roughly that same moment Matthew Arnold was earnestly erecting barricades *against* such incursions in his proclamation, held to be the founding statement of modern academic criticism, that criticism should deal only 'with the best that is known and thought in the world'. This symbolic one-on-one set the stage for a century of contestation, not only between critical discourse and the 'artistic text', but within the field of artistic practices as well. Throughout the period we know as modernism, work that was greeted with 'shock' (in other words, work that fulfilled its avant-gardist mission) was work that introduced elements of the popular, or the low, or elements untransformed by the artist's hand into the temple of Art. Synthetic cubism, which used newspapers and wallpaper in painting to destroy painting as a 'unified field'; Duchamp's ready-mades (including the infamous signed urinal); and the series of shocks and aesthetic aggressions gleefully administered by Dada and surrealism, are all examples.

Clement Greenberg, the notorious American theoretician of modernism, dismissed what he called 'kitsch', which he opposed to 'avant-garde'; he dismissed synthetic cubism to champion analytic cubism; and he termed surrealism a 're-actionary tendency' for introducing 'outside' subject matter. (Greenberg's teleology of art, emerging from his question-able use of terms like 'reactionary' or 'avant-garde', decreed a triumph of the 'pure' over mixed parentage: it is cultural miscegenation that excited his shrillest and most dictatorial denunciations.) He was still fighting these dragons through-out the sixties and well into the seventies. When confronted with proto-postmodernism in the form of minimalism, Greenberg condemned it as 'lacking aesthetic surprise' and he certainly dealt the death blow to pop art when he dismissed it as 'Novelty Art'. Greenberg was the grand master of the exclusionary shuffle – he emerges in retrospect as the hardest working man in art criticism – but in spite of his fancy foot-work the Other always threatened to close in, bringing to mind those tiny rooms where James Bond always manages to get trapped: the walls are slowly moving in, and there he stands, heroically, pectorals straining, holding them apart by sheer muscle power, mere seconds away from being squashed like an insect.[12]

IV

Even in recent serious re-theorisations of modernism, the high culture/mass culture opposition remains in place. In order to posit the existence of this aesthetic field at all, it would seem that the same exclusions must necessarily oper-ate. Peter Burger's *Theory of the Avant-Garde* (published in 1971 but only recently translated into English) attempts to rewrite the unity, modernism, into two opposing fields, first 'aestheticism' then its rival, 'the avant-garde'.

Burger first argues that the emergence of aestheticism and its challenge by the avant garde are developments in the *institutional* status of art; that the styles and contents of indi-vidual works – traditionally the site of art historical endeavours – can only be understood through the mediation of the institution of art. Secondly, he moves to reclaim the political radicality of the term 'avant-garde', against critics like Greenberg who collapse it unproblematically into modernism. For Burger, 'aestheticism', emerging in the late nineteenth century, denotes art which claims autonomy from the concerns of everyday life; form transpires to reflect this autonomy, becoming the sole content of art. In Burger's story, the avant-garde movements of the twenties began to question this autonomy and rebel against the enforced social impotence of art as determined by its institutional status. However, their move to reinsert art into the praxis of daily life failed, and Burger derides what he calls 'post-avant garde art' (singling out Warhol as his bad guy) because this work has revived techniques and procedures invented with political motives by the old avant-garde, but now uses them in a renewed aestheticism.

Interestingly though, Burger manages to place popular culture exactly where the Frankfurt School did, even while simultaneously pointing out that the relation between high and mass culture (or in his words, 'serious' and 'pulp') is not adequately thematised in their writings. He recognises that Adorno's separation of high culture and mass culture passively accepts the separation that is established within, *and establishes*, the institutions of art and literature, yet Burger himself upholds the distinction in his own dismissals of the popular. His only direct attention to mass culture yields a fairly unimaginative point about the relation between the development of photographic technology and the end of representation in painting (precisely an example of my point that high art within this period was forever running scared from the popular).

A second recent revision of modernist history is Mary Kelly's 'Re-viewing modernist criticism' in *Screen*.[13] Like Peter Burger, Kelly upholds modernist categories of the popular even while attempting to dismantle modernist ideology. She argues that modernist critical discourse functions to construct, out of disparate art practices, the category of the *artistic text*, the purpose of which is to express the essential creativity of the artistic subject. In painting, it does this by conjuring evidence of the human hand, of human action, to mark the subjectivity of the artist in artistic gesture: 'It is above all the artistic gesture which constitutes, at least metaphorically, the imaginary signifier of "Modern Art"'. The *work* of modernist critical discourse is to recover artistic subjecthood from essentially abstract work, and in a form that is fundamentally identical with the category of the bourgeois subject.

But, according to Kelly, the production of the subjective image, imperative for modernist painting, is unfeasible for narrative film, because 'the cinematic apparatus is employed to remove the traces of its own steps', while in painting, on the other hand, 'The painterly signifier is manipulated precisely to trace a passage, to give evidence of an essentially human action, to mark the subjectivity of the artist in the image itself'. The end result is 'a radical asymmetry in their respective modes of address'.

The high culture/low culture opposition is here upheld on the basis of the production of artistic subjecthood: the 'trace of a passage, or the artistic gesture' recoverable only, says Kelly, in high art. That 'the cinematic apparatus is employed to remove the traces of its own steps' is now a canonical idea within the confines of psychoanalytically inflected film criticism, but it is increasingly less self-evident in regard to contemporary film, and it should be emphasised that this theory emerged in a retrospective relation to the mass forms of high modernism – specifically, classical narrative cinema. Current cinema, though, regularly displays a variety of the formal devices of discontinuity and rupture associated with avant-gardist high art, including direct address, non-seamless modes of editing, 'making strange', etc. Current mass culture has no fear of baring the device. (Of course it would be an egregious and naïve realism to see 'truth' or value residing in *these* acts of showing the apparatus, as much as is giving great political weight to either 'materialist' practices of writing or film, or various attempts to break with ideologies of closure or identity through similarly formal disruptions.)

Moreover, '*auteur* theory' is now the most widespread informing theory in popular discourse on film, constructing the *film* as artistic text: effacing collaborative production by asserting the director as privileged artistic subject, recovering temperament, creativity, and subjectivity from the filmic text in the authorial gesture and giving it a signature. The discourse on, and of popular culture saturates us with information precisely *on* the constructedness of the motion picture, including regular 'behind the scenes' television documentaries on the making of films, like 'The Making of *Gandhi*', or the now classic 'The Making of *The Deep*'.

The techniques of modernist subjectification and the discourse of the artistic subject are not even confined to current cinema: these devices are at work in television commercials as well. Ben Yagoda claims that the only place where avant-garde theatrical techniques can still be seen is not the New York stage, but in television commercials. He finds 'an ingenious appropriation of Pirandello's musings on appearance and reality' in a commercial where a man cannot decide if he is listening to a live singer or a recording of one, then talks about it with an announcer who, it turns out, is on tape himself. And in the toilet paper advertisement which shows characters 'who seem to possess a hidden socially unacceptable urge to squeeze the merchandise', he sees the Ionescesque comedy of the absurd: 'People with ridiculous values were engaged in a ridiculous activity, which for comic effect was treated as though it were absolutely normal'. And there is the one where 'a woman about to buy the high-priced spread is cruelly browbeaten by fellow shoppers, stock boys, and the assistant manager – the Theater of Confrontation such as it hasn't been seen since the '60s'.[14]

As for the artistic subject, *auteur* theory permeates critical discourse, but it is also a marketing technique: *auteurs* now include such cinematic luminaries as Russ Meyer, the director of soft-porn epics like *Vixen* and *Beyond the Valley of the Dolls*, and Roger Corman, the oft touted 'genius' behind New World Pictures. And *auteur* theory is not confined to commercial cinema but applies now also to commercials themselves. *Esquire* magazine and others have recently run cover stories on Joe Sedelmaier, the director of the Federal Express commercials and the Wendy's 'Where's the Beef?' commercials, applying to him all the phrases *Cahiers du Cinéma* once did to Hitchcock. And the Sedelmaier commercial *is* instantly recognisable through characteristic and unique authorial gestures. *Esquire* describes him as too much his own man to go to Hollywood.

So if critical discourse produces the artistic subject for works of high art, as Mary Kelly writes, it does the same within mass culture. I would argue further that the discourse of advertising is itself constituted by this same rhetoric of imagination, rebellion, creativity and free expression that was once associated primarily with the figure of the artist. To become the quintessential artistic subject you do not have to paint your masterpiece, but only consume the right stuff. This once oppositional language, originating in the Romantic invention of the artistic subject, has achieved a dubious universality. In post-modernism, the artistic subject produced in high art, in mass culture, in advertising *and* consumption *is* the bourgeois subject. And since now the kind of claims that were once confined to the realm of high culture are freely made with regard to commodified culture and commodities themselves, we can clearly see that even areas of high culture sometimes held as critical and contestatory were always already deeply marked by these same conditions of commodification.

This indicates that the current claims of Habermas and others for a contestatory modernism are a nostalgia-ridden disavowal of the knowledge conveyed by current cultural transformations: that there is no transcendent, privileged cultural space on which to stand that is *outside* capitalist reification. There is most particularly no such space that is guaranteed strictly through particular cultural, aesthetic or textual practices: not through a refusal or disruption of the signifying practices within which subject positions are said to be constructed as suggested by *Tel Quel*, *Screen* and currently *ex cathedra* by the cultural ministry of Lacanian psychoanalysis; not through the enshrining of 'difference', or the endless and arcane formal analyses, promising, as Colin MacCabe has written, 'the absolutely new and the absolutely different, right up to the gates of the university campus'.[15]

V

The conjunction of a number of breaks has been discussed here: between modernism and postmodernism; between the remnants of an image sphere of use value and one completely permeated by commodification; between an unapproachability of popular culture and its omnipresence. The conjunction of this set of transformations meets, I would suggest, the criteria Peter Burger outlines in *Theory of the Avant-Garde*, for the possibility of a genuinely contestatory political art: one whose possible critical role is not neutralised by its institutionally determined autonomy from everyday life.

That these conditions are structurally given does not guarantee all art politically contestatory status. The artists' work described above as demonstrating the current interpenetrations of high and mass culture simply replays the categories of mass culture by 'framing' them within an art context, without in any way transforming those categories. The pleasures of this work are the pleasures of mass culture itself, despite what might be its makers' conscious intents and despite critical discourse that brands it 'oppositional'.

The set of structural possibilities and structural limits that postmodernism makes available is a field of possibility that antagonistic social forces attempt to appropriate and utilise in opposing ways. Here then is a second example of 'refunctioning' – on the other end of the political spectrum from my opening example of the transformed stop signs – an anti-abortion artwork by Mary Cate Carroll, which became newsworthy when it was barred from a show to which she had been invited at her Alma Mater, a college in Virginia. Here is the piece described in the artist's words: '. . . a 5′ x 5′ collage of a mother and father sitting on their couch. In the mother's lap is the outline – in red dotted lines – of a baby without any features. There is a door built into the middle of this baby and when you open that door there is a jar inside. A real jar, not a painting of a jar. In the jar, in formaldehyde, is a saline aborted male child. A real five-month old fetus, not a painting of a fetus'.[16] The title is *American Liberty Upside Down*.

This is certainly no original strategy: it follows the favoured tactic of anti-abortionists who like to assault women entering abortion clinics with photographs of dead foetuses. (I have been convinced that the reception of the film *E. T.* must be read in terms set by its curious echo of this contemporary iconography: the wizened figure of E. T., with its huge eyes and enlarged head, resembles nothing if not a cross between an aborted foetus and one of those Kean paintings of orphans with the great big sad eyes – making this film part of the discourse of what currently seems to be the hottest political topic in America.

But Carroll's originality, or lack of it – part of the baggage of the Romantic ideology of the artist – need not concern us here. She describes the inception of the work simply as, 'It seemed logical to me to find a fetus and put it in the painting'. The controversy began when the college told her she could not show the piece unless she replaced the real foetus with a drawing of a foetus or some other artificial substitute.

The public hue and cry about the artwork ran the gamut from 'What is art?', to the citing of laws concerning the uses to which dead bodies may or may not be put. (This last, Carroll mistakenly considered a triumph: the college invoked a state ordinance against exhibiting dead bodies as the grounds for its censorship, yet the Supreme Court opinion legalising abortion, as of this moment still in effect, defines a foetus as 'not a person'. There is an imaginary contradiciton between the two that Carroll is attempting to make a court case out of, hoping that a new court decision will actually declare her foetus a dead person.)

On the 'What is art?' question an art teacher at the college handed down her opinion that Carroll's piece *can* be considered a work of art. 'However', she says, 'the contents of a bottle that was placed on a shelf within the framework of the painting, namely a second trimester fetus, cannot by any standards be called a work of art.' She affirms the right of artists to express themselves freely but goes on, 'I do not consider human tissue to be an article of mixed media. . . What would the next step be following the display of a human fetus in a painting today? Would it be perhaps placing some other offensive morsel of human tissue, chosen by the whim of the artist, in a painting tomorrow?'

The hysterical edge provoked by Caroll's piece (note the symptomatically frequent 'fear of tissue', so reminiscent of the classic symptom-formations of earlier hysterics) testifies to the agitation-potential of self-consciously political strategies to eliminate the distance between art and the world. This strategy however in no way guarantees the reception of the work, and Carroll's piece seems not to have worked as she intended: Nat Hentoff claims that the piece was censored for the 'quintessential, visceral reason that some folks found (the fetus) disgusting', rather than an automatically convincing anti-abortion argument. Carroll wields the foetus as if it were, in itself, an objective correlative of anti-abortionism, as if, in the words of T. S. Eliot, who coined the phrase, it were 'the formula of that *particular* emotion; such that when the external facts, which must terminate in sensory experience, are given, the emotion is immediately evoked'. For Eliot, the success or failure of a piece of art rests on the 'adequacy' of the symbol or situation to the state it is meant to evoke. In these terms, Carroll's piece is inadequate, or as current terminology would put it, it is an ineffectual interpellation.

VI

The anti-abortion movement has traditionally attempted to render the foetus a totem of their movement, as if it were somehow the self-evident bearer of their position. (It has been an impossible terrain for pro-choice forces to effectively contest; they have countered by trying to shift the ground of the argument to the body of the woman.) The anti-abortion movement's strategy, clearly, is to attempt to transform the foetus into an ideological element, and appropriate it to their own discourse – through which it currently forms the basis of their ideological interpellation. (Their sophisticated understanding of exactly this point is demonstrated by their success with the film *The Silent Scream*.)

Popular culture, like the anti-abortionists' arrogation of the foetus, works by *transforming* elements at large in the culture – not through inventing or imposing arbitrary materials on a stunned and passive populace. While popular culture certainly plays a role in securing capitalist legitimation, as argued in the various versions of reproduction theory, it is not merely a siren song luring the masses onto the rocks of capitalist capitulation – with or without the unwitting complicity of their own unconscious processes. Rather, capitalist culture works by appropriating meaningful elements already extant in the culture at large – as its 'raw materials' – and transforming them in such a way that they express a capitalist hegemonic principle.

This theory of the workings of popular culture has similarities to Ernesto Laclau's analysis of populism. However, to assimilate populism to the popular culture of advanced capitalism – to return those echoes of 'the people' to the 'mass' of mass culture – is perhaps a suspect enterprise. Yet in Laclau's structural reading, populism is constituted not simply by determinate classes or determinate stages of economic development, but by a series of 'popular interpellations' which develop the antagonism between the people and the power bloc. Here, then, is a potential link between populism and popular culture.

Popular culture is not so much an instrument of domination, as an access to domination, for hegemony is not given, but always in process. Yet this is a process with cracks and openings. A class becomes hegemonic not through its capacity for sheer domination, but through its ability to interpellate both the members of its own class and members of the classes it seeks to dominate. It does this by appropriating visions of the world and diverse cultural elements of the dominated classes, but in forms which carefully neutralise any inherent or potential antagonism. Typically those antagonisms are transformed into a simple *difference* (hence 'liberal pluralism'), in a process of absorption and neutralisation of those ideological contents of the dominated classes through which resistance to domination might be expressed. Classes only exist as hegemonic forces to the extent that they can appropriate popular interpellations to their own discourse, but in an articulation which neutralises 'the people' as an oppositional force.

This argument locates the work of popular culture somewhat closer to the level of the conscious subject – perhaps Freud's term 'preconscious' would apply here – than do most recent theorisations of mass culture, which find capitalist legitimation secured in a deeply recessed and unavailable unconsciousness – that mist-enshrouded primordial mating ground of signifying practices and anatomical difference.

That particular location, I would argue, effectively forecloses in advance the significance of any cultural practice other than the most ultra-modernist.

The theory of postmodernism presented here argues for a different cultural practice. Dismissing popular culture as merely an instrument of capitalist domination, rather than a site to be struggled over, simply cedes the territory of popular interpellation to capitalism. Certainly much of the success of capitalist hegemony comes from its exclusive claim to those elements in the culture that are socially meaningful (like *narrative*) and its transformation of those elements into the basis of the continuing appeal of an existing social order. According to Laclau, for the dominated classes to win hegemony they must precipitate a crisis in the dominant ideological discourse, stripping the connotative power from its articulating principles. For this to happen the implicit antagonism of those popular interpellations must be developed to the point where 'the people' are not available for assimilation by any fraction of the power bloc.

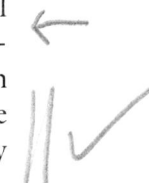

Much capitalist popular culture obviously already expresses antagonism to 'the system' – anti-government, anti-corporate, and anti-technology themes are far from rare. A left popular culture would undertake to articulate the antagonistic moments *already* there in popular culture into moments when 'popular-democratic' elements are presented as an unassimilable option *against* the ideology of the dominant bloc – not mere 'difference' cosily embraced under the umbrella of a happy liberal pluralism and comprising part of its ongoing public relations for itself. Laclau refers to this as the 'ideological class struggle': the attempt to articulate the same interpellations in antagonistic discourses. This strategy aims to provoke a crisis of the dominant ideological discourse and a crisis in the ability of the system to neutralise its dominated sectors: this, in Laclau's version of populism, precipitating a more general social crisis. Precisely because 'the people' can never be *totally* absorbed by any dominant class

discourse, the articulation of an antagonistic moment characterises populism: and the more radical the confrontation with
the system, the less possible is it for a class to assert its
hegemony without populism.

VII

A left popular culture is here synonymous with populism, a
political mobilisation posing a challenge to capitalist
hegemony, and without which no such challenge can be
made. It must be said that this proposal of a conjunction
between a left popular culture and populism is aimed more
specifically toward formulating a strategy for the production
of a left popular culture, rather than toward fostering critical
stategies that provide readings of the antagonisms inherent
in already existing popular culture. This has marked the general limit of left involvement with popular culture; the render-
ing of interpretations which are produced and circulate
within the circumscribed domains of high culture and high
theory.[17]

The focus on producing a left popular culture also accounts
for the emphasis here towards conscious experience. This is
not necessarily a theoretical bias in favour of ego psychology
or American revisionism over continental psychoanalysis –
two poles of ongoing polemic in left film theory – and it is
not intended to merely dismiss important psychoanalytically
derived theories on production of the subject within popular
cultural forms. Rather, the focus on conscious experience is
provisional, part of a provisional strategy for a provisional
postmodernist cultural politics of 'refunctioning'.

What I have intended to do is to interrogate the forms in
which culture and cultural politics are inevitably produced
by, on the one hand, privileging the unconscious, and on
the other, stressing the insurmountable and delusion-pro-
ducing monoliths bred in the interfaces of a repressive social
order and practices of signification. These emphases work

to produce and determine a particular *representation* of a cultural field, and one which bodes ill for left intervention. It is this representation that legislates the inevitability of arcane and academicist interpretations of popular culture which impute diminished intellectual and political credibility to its audience; this representation which produced the certainty of an elitist high culture; and this representation which assures the endless repetition of modernist sterilities as an imaginary antidote to the worldly hurly-burly of capitalist popular culture. It would seem that the only politics that can result from such a representation just revivifies the corner that Adorno painted himself into: political hibernation.

Both theorists of modernism and theorists of the unconscious have recoiled from popular culture, whether in attempting to interpret it, to defy it, or to purge it. The point of the populist intervention suggested here, however, is to change it.

Notes

1 I would like to thank Jonathan Arac for help with both versions of the paper on which this chapter is based.

2 Louis Althusser, 'Ideology and Ideological State Apparatuses', in *'Lenin and Philosophy and Other Essays* (New York: Monthly Review Press, 1971).

3 Reported by CBS News from the 1984 Republican Convention.

4 WALTER BENJAMIN, *Understanding Brecht* (London: New Left Books, 1973), pp. 93-4.

5 Ernesto Laclau, *Politics and Ideology in Marxist Theory* (London: New Left Books, 1977). See also Chantel Mouffe, 'Hegemony and ideology in Gramsci', in her *Gramsci and Marxist Theory* (London: Routledge and Kegan Paul, 1979).

6 Raymond Williams, *Keywords* (New York: Oxford University Press, 1976), pp. 158-63.

7 PETER BURGER, *Theory of the Avant-Garde* (Manchester: Manchester University Press, 1984).

8 Michael Taussig, *The Devil and Commodity Fetishism in South America* (Chapel Hill: University of North Carolina Press, 1980).

9 See ERNEST MANDEL, *Late Capitalism* (London: New Left Books, 1975), p. 191.

10 Laclau, 'Toward a theory of populism', in *op. cit.,* pp. 143-98.

11 Guy Debord, *Society of the Spectacle* (Detroit: Black and Red, 1977).

12 Clement Greenberg, 'Avant-Garde and Kitsch' in *Art and Culture: Critical Essays* (Boston: Beacon Press, 1964); 'The Necessity of Formalism', *The Lugano Review*, October 1972; and 'The recentness of sculpture', *American*

Sculpture of the Sixties exhibition catalogue, (Los Angeles County Museum of Art, 1967).

13 Mary Kelly, 'Re-viewing modernist critisism', *Screen*, (22, 3, 1981).

14 Ben Yagoda, 'Don't squeeze the Ionesco', *The Village Voice*, (4 December 1978), p. 66.

15 Colin MacCabe, 'Coming down: elements of an intellectual autobio-graphy', in *Tracking the Signifier*, University of Minnisota Press, 1985.

16 Nat Hentoff, 'If it's not a human being, what's the crime?', *The Village Voice*, (6 March 1984) p. 6.

17 Frederic Jameson's 'Reification and Utopia in mass culture', *Social Text* 1, 1979, while certainly high theory, is an exception in that it is also a political intervention, and its argument is important to my treatment of popular culture. I have drawn heavily as well from Jameson's work on postmodernism (although I suspect he is less sanguine than I am here about the possibilities for a contes-tatory postmoderism). See, for example, his 'Postmodernism and consumer society' in *The Anti-Aesthetic*, ed., Hal Foster (Port Townsend: Bay Press, 1983).

Femininity as mas(s)querade: a feminist approach to mass culture

In closing remarks given at the weekend seminar on popular culture John Caughie referred in passing to an 'absence of feminist work around popular culture'. Another participant, Simon Frith, pointed out that women have indeed addressed questions of popular culture, but that when women talk about it, it is not generally considered popular culture. Frith referred to Rosalind Coward's book *Female Desire*, which analyses fashions, romances, women's magazines, and a whole host of specifically feminine cultural artifacts and practices. In effect, he was pointing to the critical double standard which has been as pervasive in popular culture studies as it has been in studies of high culture – a double standard I discuss in the first chapter of my own work on women and popular culture, *Loving with a Vengeance: Mass-produced Fantasies for Women*. Although women have spoken, then, they have not always been heard, and one of the tasks for feminism is continually to insist upon recognition, as well as upon the priority of its work.

Beyond this important role that must be assigned to feminist criticism, however, lies an even larger role – the necessity of showing that the entire issue of gender is of much larger significance than has previously been acknowledged in discussions of mass culture. Gender has typically been theorised as simply one positioning among many, one possible point of resistance to mass culture's attempts to homogenise social reality. Thus Fredric Jameson says:

The only authentic cultural production today has seemed to be that which can draw on the collective experience of marginal pockets of the social life of the world system: black literature and blues, British working-class rock, women's literature, gay literature, the *roman québecois*, the literature of the Third World; and this production is possible only to the degree to which these forms of collective life or collective solidarity have not yet been fully penetrated by the market and by the commodity system.[1]

Orthodox Marxism today abandons its exclusive reliance on the working class as agents of revolutionary change, and grants women and a few other groups a token importance as well. The invocation of the women's movement occurs towards the end of an essay with no feminist perspective, and women are brought in at the last to be offered as one of the few rays of hope in what has been portrayed as a bleak situation. Indeed, the very measure of its bleakness, it is implied, is that women, gays, and rock groups – these 'marginal pockets' of social life – *are* our best hope.

But the issue of gender in relation to mass culture goes much deeper and ramifies in a number of quite surprising directions. By looking at several different kinds of discourse, I want to show how our ways of thinking and feeling about mass culture are so intricately bound up with notions of the feminine that the need for a feminist critique becomes obvious at every level of the debate. To begin with, women find themselves at the centre of many historical accounts of mass culture, damned as 'mobs of scribbling women', in Hawthorne's famous phrase, and held responsible for the debasement of taste and the sentimentalisation of culture. As the example of Hawthorne suggests, historians of culture are not the only ones who blame women for creating the conditions of what Ann Douglas calls 'the cultural sprawl that has increasingly characterised post-Victorian life'.[2] Artists themselves adopt this view, which holds such sway not because of its truth value but because it rests on powerful stereotypes, habits of language, and unexamined – because unconscious – psychic associations.

In this chapter I want first to examine the orthodox position of the literary historian for the way in which mass culture is condemned as a 'feminised' culture. Then I will discuss the work of two other contemporaries, an artist (Manuel Puig) and a theorist (Jean Baudrillard) who, far from condemning mass culture because it is 'effeminate', try to re-evaluate and to some extent affirm it precisely on the grounds of its association with or resemblance to the feminine. This is certainly an interesting twist to the old debate, though it must be remembered that the feminine has always been a term alternately denigrated and exalted. Whether the latest development represents a gain for women or for feminism remains to be seen.

The orthodox view can be found in its sternest form in *The Feminization of American Culture* by critic, literary historian, and professed feminist, Ann Douglas. The book was a major publishing event and a resounding critical success in America. The New York *Times* called it 'indispensable reading for modern feminists', as if most feminists were not already familiar with the account it gives of a few male champions of high culture waging an heroic but losing battle against the onslaught of those effete sentimentalisers of culture – women writers and their clerical allies. With all the fervour of one converted to, rather than born in the patriarchal faith, Douglas not only judges the writings of the majority of nineteenth-century women to be of inferior quality when measured against the artistic achievements of a Herman Melville; she also holds them entirely accountable for the advent of modern mass culture. Discussing Little Eva in Harriet Beecher Stowe's *Uncle Tom's Cabin* as the archetypal heroine of women's fiction and Little Eva's death as the archetypal event, Douglas writes:

(Stowe's infantile heroine anticipates that exaltation of the average
(which is the trademark of mass culture. Vastly superior as she is
to most of her figurative offspring, she is nonetheless the childish
predecessor of Miss America, of 'Teen Angel', of the ubiquitous,
everyday, wonderful girl about whom thousands of popular songs
and movies have been made. . . In a sense, my introduction to
Little Eva and to the Victorian scenes, objects and sensibility of
which she is suggestive was my introduction to consumerism. The
pleasure Little Eva gave me provided historical and practical preparation for the equally indispensable and disquieting comforts of
mass culture. (2-3)

Instigating the Civil War was obviously not the last charge
for which Stowe would be answerable. Despite Douglas's
homage in the book to a masculine kind of intellectual 'tough-
ness', what is remarkable about this passage is its reliance on
impressionistic associations. Out of such associations are
generated a causal sequence and a history. The last line of
the passage is ironic in the light of Douglas's repeated casti-
gations of the woman for their narcissism, of which Little
Eva is the chief examplar. Somehow Douglas's private
pleasure metamorphoses into an *ex post facto* 'historical preparation' for the national and increasingly global phenomenon of mass culture itself. Nowhere does she consider the
question of who profits from Miss America, not does she
acknowledge the extent to which the image of the 'teen angel'
antedates Stowe and the vast majority of women writers.

Little Eva's death from 'consumption' would appear to
take on a retroactively symbolic signficance. But rather than
examine the forces that conspire to condemn women to be
the pre-eminent consumers in consumer society, the literary
historian often assumes women's habit of consumption to
be nearly as unavoidable as death. In an illuminating passage,
Douglas remarks that 'content was *not* the most important
aspect of their work. Ministerial and feminine authors were
as involved with the method of consumption as with the
article consumed'. Thus, in an extraordinary move, Douglas

manages to transform even women's production of texts into an act of consumption, or, in Roland Barthes' terminology, their writing of books into a readerly practice.

Douglas goes on to contrast the nineteenth-century minister, who preferred 'light reading' (i.e. fiction and poetry), to the well-educated eighteenth-century minister of Calvinism (a religion that she elsewhere admits 'was repressive, authoritarian, dogmatic, patriarchal to an extreme'(12)). The latter read 'dense argumentative tracts' that 'forced him to think, not to "read" in our modern sense; metaphorically speaking, he was producing, not consuming'. Finally, Douglas speaks of the 'countless Victorian women' who 'spent much of their middle-class girlhoods prostrate on chaise-longues with their heads buried in "worthless novels"'. Douglas's evidence is taken from the writings of contemporary 'observers' contrasting these girls unfavourably with their supposedly more industrious grandmothers who 'spent their time studying the Bible and performing useful household chores'. Now, 'evidence' of this kind should clearly be treated with considerable caution by the tough-minded historian. But it is not the truth value of these observations that counts. It is the vivid *image* of girls prostrate on chaise-longues, immersed in their worthless novels, that has provided historical preparation for the practice of countless critics who persist in equating femininity, consumption, and reading, on the one hand, and masculinity, production, and writing on the other.

The wilfulness of these connections is indicated by the fact that Douglas singles out Stowe's *Uncle Tom's Cabin* (the book which was said to have produced a war) to indict for introducing the pleasures of consumerism. Far from being a work that simply participates in a kind of 'complicated mass dream life', which for Douglas means that such books are readerly even in their writing, recent criticism has shown how carefully crafted and controlled the novel actually is. Moreover, feminist analysis has revealed that its Utopian vision is based upon an ideal of *feminine* production in the home which gets extended into an ideal for national and international government. As Jane Tompkins notes, the home 'is conceived as a dynamic center of activity, physical and spiritual, economic and moral, whose influence spreads out in ever widening circles'.[3] Feminist criticism of this sort leads us to re-evaluate and clarify our terms and to rid our selves of some of the unconscious associations they carry. Too often politically-oriented criticism invokes 'production' as an ideal pure and simple, without concerning itself with what is being produced. Thus, the Calvinist minister is praised for 'producing the texts he read', even though they may have been 'repressive, authoritarian, dogmatic, patriarchal in the extreme'. On the other hand, Stowe is condemned for allowing readers to become 'absorbed' in her thrilling novel (i.e. to consume it) despite the fact that she was presenting them with an ideology based upon a feminine mode of production and intended 'to effect a radical transformation of. . . society'.[4] Such a view exposes the masculinist bias of much politically-oriented criticism that adopts metaphors of production and consumption in order to differentiate between progressive and regressive activities of reading (or viewing, as the case may be).

Tompkins's strategy is to correct this masculinist bias by expanding the definition of 'production' to include the kind of work that women do. An alternative strategy might consist of deconstructing the hierarchical relation that exists in the oppositions production/consumption and writerly/readerly in order to search out the radical potential of the subordinate terms, each of which, as we have seen, is typically associated with the feminine. Indeed, as one might expect in our post-modern age, such a project has already been initiated by artists and theorists alike.

Manuel Puig's acclaimed novel *Kiss of the Spider Woman* provides an excellent example of such a deconstuctive text. The novel takes place in an Argentinian prison where the homosexual 'queen' Molina helps pass the time by relating film plots to his cellmate, a Marxist revolutionary named Valentin. The setting of the novel obviously gives new meaning to the usually pejorative designation of mass-produced art as 'escapist'. The novel draws on the conventions of the prison film, only here the films themselves function as 'the great escape'.

Kiss of the Spider Woman is the story of the growing love of Valentin for Molina, although this is rendered obliquely, since the book presents us primarily with the dialogue between the two. At the beginning of the book the men tend to disagree and quarrel a great deal, but they gradually come to know and like each other better, largely as a result of their discussions about films which frequently provoke personal associations and revelations. Molina has been bribed by the prison warden to elicit information about Valentin's political activities in return for his parole. He appears to go along with the plan, yet it becomes clear that he is doing so for his own purposes: thus he manages to procure food from the warden (so Valentin will not be suspicious of his absence from the cell when he is brought out by the warden but will simply assume that his mother has come to see him), and he uses this food to 'soften up' Valentin for the seduction that finally occurs. At the end, the warden changes his tactics and releases Molina in the hopes that he will lead them to Valentin's comrades. And this is precisely what happens, since Valentin has extracted a promise from Molina to deliver a message to his cohorts, who, possibly because they spot the police when they arrive at the designated meeting place, gun him down in the street. Subsequently, Valentin is tortured, a merciful doctor gives him some drugs, and he has a dream constructed out of the images and plots of the films Molina has described throughout the book.

At the beginning of the novel, although Valentin very much enjoys indulging in the 'escapist' pleasures offered him by Molina, he deeply distrusts this enjoyment and insists on restricting the storytelling to bedtime, for he adopts the standard leftist view of popular culture. Not unlike Douglas's Calvinist minister, Valentin forces himself to struggle with his difficult political science tracts, repudiating the attractions of the film stories. 'It can become a vice, always trying to escape from reality like that, it's like taking drugs or something. . . If you read something, if you study something, you transcend any cell you're inside of, do you understand what I'm saying?'[5] At one point, Valentin condemns himself for his 'weakness' in becoming attached to the characters in one of the stories and feeling sad that the 'film' has ended (41). It becomes clear that Valentin associates this 'weakness' with femininity and fears the passivity involved in the processes of identification and empathy – those *bêtes noires* of Marxist literary and film criticism. Surrendering oneself *to* the texts is to assume an uncomfortable resemblance to the women *in* the texts – for example, the zombie woman, who is powerless to resist the will of others, even though it means burning herself alive at her husband's command.

It is to assume, as well, an uncomfortable resemblance to Molina, who, as the consumer *par excellence*, yields himself to the films with utter abandon, resents Valentin's attempts to analyse the stories, and weeps when Valentin criticises his favourite film, which is, significantly, a Nazi propaganda film that he admires for its aesthetic beauty and for the love story. Furthermore, Molina's attitude towards men, like his attitude towards films, is one of complete surrender of self. For example, he tells Valentin of a fantasy he has of living with a waiter with whom he is infatuated. He dreams of helping him study and arranging things so that the man will never have to work again. 'And I'd pass along whatever small amount of money was needed to give the wife for child support, and make him not worry about anything at all, nothing except himself, until he got what he wanted and lost all that sadness of his for good, wouldn't that be marvelous?' (69).

Having set up the traditional polarities that we saw were

operative in Douglas's work (masculine = production and work; feminity = consumption and passivity), Puig proceeds to effect a transvaluation of the terms. The project of the novel is to get Valentin to accept the otherness that Molina represents – femininity, homosexuality, and mass culture – and, ultimately to allow himself to be sexually and textually seduced by Molina, whom he calls 'the spider woman'. The spider woman is featured in the drug-induced dream Valentin has at the end of the book: at first she appears to Valentin to be trapped in a spider's web, but then it becomes clear that the spider's web is growing out of her own body, 'the threads are coming out of her waist and hips, they're part of her body, so many threads that look like hairy ropes and disgust me, even though if I were to touch them they might feel as smooth as who knows what, but it makes me queasy to touch them. . .' (280). The description of the spider woman, an image of femininity and of homosexuality taken from mass culture, suggests what is at stake in Valentin's attitude toward his others: the fear of entrapment and absorption, which is simultaneously desired and dreaded.

Throughout the novel Puig is satirising traditional Marxism in the figure of Valentin, and in both the narrative and the accompanying footnotes, the book indicates that a revolution must occur in the personal realm as well as the political and must be concerned with sex and gender as well as class. For Marxism, which is classically preoccupied with production, this sexual revolution would involve a new and more positive attitude towards consumption. Hence the book's obsessive concern with food. Valentin at first resists being nurtured by Molina, as he resists the film stories. Finally, however, he comes to accept the various consumer pleasures offered and embodied by Molina and changes his mind about the importance of 'sensory gratification' which he earlier repudiated. At the beginning, for example, he protests that Molina's cooking and storytelling is getting him into 'bad habits':

There's no way I can live for the moment because my life is dedicated to political struggle. . . Social revolution, that's what's important, and gratifying the senses is only secondary. The great pleasure's something else, it's knowing I've put myself in the service of a noble. . . ideology. . . Marxism. . . And I can get that pleasure anywhere, right here in this cell and even in torture. (27-8)

One of the ironies of Valentin's manifesto is his lack of awareness that his machismo contains strong elements of passivity and even masochism (pleasure in torture). Thus the traits that Valentin rejects as feminine are revealed early in the novel to be important parts of his character. By the end, Valentin has been reduced to helplessness at the hands of Molina, who feeds him, wipes and bathes him after he has been incontinent, and continues to tell him films at bedtime 'like lullabies' (279). He learns to view his 'weaknesses' as less shameful and, at least to a certain extent, comes to enjoy being submissive.

As for Molina, his identification with the passive and often masochistic heroines of his films, his swooning rapture over the films he describes, would appear to make him the ideal manipulated consumer. On the contrary, however, it becomes increasingly apparent as the novel progresses that Molina uses the films in order to do his own manipulating. On occasion he admits to resorting to strategy, as when he confesses that he likes to leave Valentin 'hanging' so he will enjoy the film more. 'You have to do it that way with the public, otherwise they're not satisfied. On the radio they always used to do that to you. And now on the T.V. soaps' (25-6). In other words, Molina uses the techniques of manipulation he has learned from his adored mass culture in order to seduce Valentin into his web. Mass culture becomes not the enemy, as it is for the Marxist, but the very agency through which Molina accomplishes his coup and conquers Valentin. The triumph that Molina achieves precisely through his utter devotion both to men and to the films, as

well as by his apparent submission to the law represented by
the warden, is attributable to what Jean Baudrillard, quoting
Hegel, calls 'the eternal irony of femininity' that supposedly
characterises the masses – 'the irony of a false fidelity to the
law, an ultimately impenetrable simulation of passivity and
obedience. . . which in return annuls the law governing
them'.[6] Molina's exaggeration of the feminine – his simulation of womanhood, derived from emulating film heroines,
realises an ideal of femininity as mas(s)querade: the homosexual 'queen' as exemplar of the hyperreal.

In the above passage, taken from *In the Shadow of the Silent
Majorities or the Death of the Social*, Baudrillard himself is
justifying the masses, rather than condemning them on
account of their putative femininity. This is the only reference
to the feminisation of culture in the entire work, and yet it
is crucial, for the essay builds upon this Hegelian notion of
feminine seduction, which is really a synonym for that very
fashionable term introduced by Baudrillard: 'simulation'. (It
is more than coincidence that Baudrillard has authored an
entire book on the subject of feminine seduction.) Thus, the
word 'simulation' itself dissimulates, masking the extent to
which Baudrillard's theorisation of the masses and mass culture duplicates the theorisation of the feminine in much contemporary thought.

Just as Molina refuses to accept Valentin's analyses of the
films ('why break the illusion for me, and for yourself
too?'(17)), Baudrillard's masses resist the intellectual's
attempts to impose on them 'the imperative of rational communication' (10). Instead, they demand spectacle; they prefer
to be fascinated rather than provoked to thought. Thus far,
of course, Baudrillard is in complete agreement with most
critics of mass culture. He differs from them crucially, however, in placing a positive value on the masses' refusal of
meaning. Again like Molina, whose ingenuousness continually exposes Valentin's Marxist priciples as narrow and inflex-
ible, the masses, according to Baudrillard, 'scent the simplify-

ing terror which is behind the ideal hegemony of meaning' (10). Baudrillard here aligns himself with various contemporary thinkers, like Roland Barthes, who implicitly denounces the terrorism of the 'hegemony of meaning' when he speaks of 'regime of meaning'.[7] Barthes, however, considers this regime to be in the service of mass culture and repeatedly calls on high art to challenge and overthrow it. For Baudrillard, on the contrary, the *masses* are in the best position to answer Barthes' call; they 'realise here and now everything which the most radical critics have been able to envisage', as they 'wander through meaning, the political, representation, history, ideology, with a somnambulant strength of denial'(49). They annihilate everything that seeks to control them, not by their strength of will but by their very will-lessness and passivity.

The masses function as a 'gigantic black hole', a simile ostensibly taken from physics, but perhaps owing something to (feminine) anatomy as well: 'an implosive sphere', a 'sphere of potential engulfment' (9). According to Baudrillard, the rabid consumerism suggested by the term 'engulfment' is truly radical in its potential. For 'a system is abolished only by pushing it into hyperlogic. . . You want us to consume – O.K. let's consume always more, and anything whatsoever; for any useless and absurd purpose' (46). Here the values espoused by Ann Douglas and other traditional leftist thinkers are completely reversed. Meaning, regardless of who 'produces' it or how, is explosive and terroristic; consumption is implosive and revolutionary. (At least, it *may* be revolutionary. Baudrillard is aware of the fact that this implosive tendency of the 'somnambulant' masses means that they are likely enough to destroy themselves in destroying the system, like the zombie woman who has to burn herself alive in order to eradicate the evil that possesses the village.)

And, as we have seen, Baudrillard, unlike Douglas, is far from denigrating the putative femininity of mass culture. The masses who push the system into a hyperlogic are

engaging in the same 'excessive fidelity to the law' that characterises Hegel's eternal feminine, the same 'simulation of passivity and obedience' that 'annuls the law governing them'.
It is the mute acquiescence of the masses to the system – the
silence of the majority – that renders them most feminine.
The masses, outside of meaning, are outside of language and
of representation: hence the end of politics as we know it.
'Withdrawn into their silence. . . they can no longer be
spoken for, articulated, represented, nor pass through the
political "mirror" stage, and the cycle of imaginary identifications' (22). Baudrillard here is extending contemporary
psychoanalytic definitions of woman to a political analysis
of the masses. For in current theory it is *woman* who has
been consigned to silence because of her inability to pass
through the mirror stage, to enter language, the symbolic
and the social. Thus she had been called 'the ruin of repre
sentation'. In her 'formlessness' she can only, paradoxically,
represent lack – that is, the horrible possibility of *un*repre
sentability, the 'abyss' or 'void' of meaning, to use Baudrillard's term.

Declaring the masses to be the ruin of (political) representation, Baudrillard rather gleefully and apocalyptically proclaims the death of the social. In former times, 'the devices
of classic sociality' ensured that 'social meaning still flows
between one pole and another'. But with the devices of 'simulation' there is 'no longer any pole nor any differential term,
hence no electricity of the social either: it is short-circuited
by the confusing of poles, in a total circularity of signalling'
(21). In another essay Baudrillard makes clear that such 'circularity of signalling' characteristic of our electronic age
means the end of both domestic space and the public sphere.
On the one hand, television (for example) exposes the privacy
of domestic space to the scrutiny of the entire world (as in
the case of the Loud family); while, on the other hand, all
the events of the universe unfold nightly on our private television screens. The individual experiences 'this forced

extroversion of all interiority, this forced injection of all exteriority' as a kind of rape: 'the unclean promiscuity of everything which touches, invests and penetrates without resistance, with no halo of private protection, not even his own body to protect him any more'.[8] Once again, then, the masses are shown to be utterly feminised in their mediatisation: in the past, of course, it was woman who was forced to live the loss of both public and private space – denied participation in the public sphere, and, though confined to domesticity, forbidden real privacy (a room of her own) and even legal possession of her body.

Baudrillard's work has recently had an enormous impact not only on mass culture theory but on art criticism as well. To take only one example, *ZG*, a journal of art criticism, recently published a special issue on the subject of 'the body'. Throughout the issue, which contains several articles that are feminist in intent, the writers quote Baudrillard as the ultimate authority, exhibiting an 'excessive fidelity' to the theory that, not surprisingly, does nothing to 'annul' its power. It is important for feminists to draw out and scrutinise the implications of Baudrillard's conceptualisation of the masses and mass culture, and in particular to question its significance for feminism. Feminists disturbed by contemporary theory's relegation of women to the realm of the presocial might be tempted to rejoice prematurely in the end of the social and the consignment of almost *everyone* to the place hitherto reserved for women. But that would be to gloss over crucial distinctions.

In an important essay that is useful for my purposes, Nancy Miller questions the relevance to feminism of Foucault's work on the death of the author. She argues that contrary to what some feminists have claimed, it is Foucault's 'sovereign indifference' to the matter of 'who's speaking', and not the concept of authorship itself, that is the mask 'behind which phallocentrism hides its fictions':

. . . the authorising function of its own discourse authorises the 'end of woman' without consulting her. What matter who's speaking? I would answer that it matters, for example, to women who have lost and still routinely lose their proper name in marriage, and whose signature. . . has not been worth the paper it was written on; women for whom signature – by virtue of its power in the world of circulation – is *not* immaterial. Only those who have it can play with not having it.[9]

The death of the social is another of phallocentrism's masks, likewise authorising the 'end of woman' without consulting her: 'the social itself no longer has any name. Anonymous. THE MASS. THE MASSES' (19). Only those who have had privileged access to the social can gleefully announce its demise. For women, who throughout most of history have not been given political representation or a political voice – a state of affairs that has made them the *true* silent majority – there is little reason to be sanguine about the possibilities of a revolution based on the mute tactics of the eternal 'feminine'.

Not the least of the problems involved in equating the masses and mass culture with the feminine is that it becomes much more difficult for women to interrogate their role within that culture. As Freud put it in his essay on 'Femininity' (employing patriarchal strategies of deviousness), if women *are* the question, they cannot *ask* the questions. And yet it is crucial for us to ask them, because, as feminist critics have begun to show, women are victimised in many and complex ways in mass culture. Valentin was undoubtedly right the first time: the spider woman *was* in fact entrapped in that web, as almost all the women in the movies Molina discusses are ensnared in various patriarchal traps, and as Molina himself is destroyed at the end, letting 'himself be killed because that way he could die like some heroine in a movie'(279).

Despite the suggestion in *Kiss of the Spider Woman* of a role reversal and a shift in power dynamics – with Molina temporarily in the ascendency as a result of his feminine strategies, which are also the strategies of the consumer – nothing much ever really changes. Throughout, Molina remains in the feminine role of nurturer and caretaker, while Valentin reaps all the benefits of consumerism (nobody feeds Molina or tells him stories). And despite Baudrillard's implicit denial of the contemporary relevance of sexual difference, as all difference and all politics – including feminist politics – are supposedly absorbed into a feminised mass, women daily experience a sense of oppression in a social order that is at least alive enough to ensure the continuance of that oppression. A feminist approach to mass culture might begin, then, by recognising and challenging the dubious sexual analogies that pervade a wide variety of dis courses, however seductive they may at first appear. And this is especially important when, as in the case of Baudrillard, such discourses masquerade as theories of liberation.

Notes

1 Frederic Jameson, 'Reification and utopia in mass culture', *Social Text* 1, 1979, p. 148.

2 Ann Douglas, *The Feminization of American Culture* (New York: Avon, 1977), p. 13. All further references are to this edition.

3 Jane P. Tompkins, 'Sentimental power: *Uncle Tom's Cabin* and the politics of literary history', *Glyph* 8, 1981, p. 98. Tompkins is directly responding to Douglas's book.

4 *Ibid.*

5 Manuel Puig, *Kiss of the Spider Woman*, trans. Thomas Colchie (New York: Vintage, 1980), p. 78. All further references are to this edition.

6 Jean Baudrillard, *In the Shadow of the Silent Majorities or the End of the Social and Other Essays*, trans. Paul Foss, Paul Patton and John Johnston (New York: Semiotexte, 1983), p. 33. All further references are to this edition.

7 Roland Barthes, *Image, Music Text*, trans. Stephen Heath (New York: Hill and Wang, 1977), p. 167.

8 Jean Baudrillard, 'The ecstasy of communication', trans. John Johnston, in *The Anti-Aesthetic*, ed. Hal Foster (Port Townsend: Bay Press, 1983), p. 132.

9 Nancy K. Miller, 'The text's heroine: a feminist critic and her fictions', *Diacritics*, summer 1982, p. 53.

Hearing secret harmonies

The Polish musicologist Zofia Lissa has written that 'silent' films needed, in fact, to be accompanied by music for a variety of reasons – to cover the noise of the projector and the passing traffic, to maintain or switch moods more smoothly than early cutting and editing devices could, to give early cinema a veneer of respectability – but the point she makes that most interests me is that silence in a cinema is embarrassing.[1] This is obviously true nowadays – to show students silent films on a course is to call forth a shuffle of nervous feet, stifled giggles, stagy whispers – and it suggests one of the central use of popular music in this century: to conceal the furtive pleasure of indulging in private fantasies in public places.

In this chapter, I want to examine some of the ways in which film music works, but I must begin by setting my remarks in the framework of a more general comment on popular culture.

'Popular culture' describes culture in capitalist societies (elsewhere, 'folk culture' or even just 'culture' are adequate terms) and the most common way of looking at popular culture is therefore in terms of the production and consumption of commodities. The recurring twentieth-century question has been what is the relationship of 'art' and the market place; the recurring answer has been in terms of the opposition between high culture and mass culture – the place of popular culture in this couplet is unclear. One reason for this is that the high/mass culture typology actually muddles two

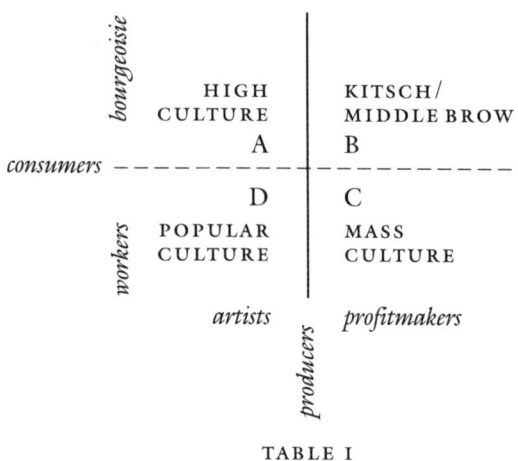

TABLE I

issues, production and consumption. This can be clarified by Table 1.

Most sociology is focused on A (high culture) and C (mass culture) but boxes B and D are equally interesting, especially given how thin most of the dividing lines really are. High culture very easily becomes middlebrow culture (the general move of the classical music tradition this century); mass culture and middlebrow culture are no more easily distinguished (how should Andrew Lloyd Webber's *Requiem* be classified?) than mass culture and popular culture, the usual focus for left-wing debate. At first glance the distinction between A and D, high and popular culture, seems sharper, but even here there are problems – how should post-war jazz be classified? the popular avant-garde more generally? All this table does is reveal how confident aesthetic judgements (A and D are good; B and C are bad) rest on muddled aesthetic categories. My approach to popular culture depends, then, on scrapping this typology entirely. The concept 'mass culture', in particular, is supect both theoretically and historically. I prefer the notion of 'capitalist culture' – culture defined, that is, not in terms of the production and consumption of commodities (though this is involved) but as the way in which people deal with/symbolise/articulate/share/resist the *experience* of capitalism (including, but not exclusively, the ideological experience of capitalism). From this perspective the most important quality of capital is that it is in a state of premanent crisis; the experience of capitalism means, as Marshall Berman has argued, the exprience of modernity. The logic of capital accumulation is a logic of cultural dynamism; divisions of labour and the labour process itself keep changing, as live labour is replaced by the dead labour embodied in machines; a constant flow of new products means the continual arousal of new needs. The contradiction of capitalist culture is that the need for social reproduction means a simultaneous emphasis on ideological stability, on tradition, history, established morality, common sense (hence the key significance of the family). For individuals living with capitalism, three 'issues of experience' need constant handling: (a) *issues of change and continuity* (think of the role of nostalgia in the mass media, from pop records to video games, its combination with fashion, novelty and 'progress'. Popular memory is one of the most important products of popular culture; popular pleasures involve experiences of both integration and disintegration); (b) *issues of identification and difference;* and (c) *issues of activity and passivity.*

Following up issues (b) and (c) it is clear that both high and popular culture are aspects of capitalist culture (and can only be understood in relationship to each other). Their distinction is not clean-cut and shifts historically – if high culture has, on the whole, been used to articulate ruling class and bourgeois identify, popular culture has not generally just expressed working-class concerns – the *petit-bourgeoisie* and middle classes have had a crucial role in developing popular forms, in determining, that is, the ways in which culture produces poeple's sense of identity, their sense of who they are, where they belong. Popular culture produces 'the people', not vice versa, and, in subjective terms, what seems to be involved here is not identification as such (between fan and star, say) but a process of *recognition,* in which cultural form – tones of voice, jokiness, parody, a self-conscious distancing, *play* with relationships of fantasy and reality – is as important as cultural content (this is certainly apparent in British popular culture, from children's comics to rock music to television 'soaps' and the daily press).

'Taste' involves, by definition, the idea of shared taste; to choose a programme or a record is to be like other people who choose that programme or record – this is part of what such choices are about (and choice differentiates one from people with different tastes too). All popular culture involves shared experience, however 'privatised' it seems; the tired contrast between the collective activity of watching a football match and the individual activity of watching television is indeed meaningless. It is through popular culture that we discover what shared experience means – hence the *Minder* effect (in south London, everyone now talks like Terry and Arthur) and more generally, the recurring phenomena of media cults. The most important ideological role of capitalist culture is to mobilise people to vote or to buy by 'placing' them, giving them a social identity through popular taste. What we need, as socialists, is a much clearer understanding of how this mobilisation works *and* fails, under what circumstances cultural forms have an oppositional effect.

In this context the public/private distinction common in cultural sociology is hard to maintain. People do not have 'private' knowledge, particularly not private emotional

knowledge, knowledge independent of public cultural meanings and experiences (think again, of the concept of 'taste',
something that is not exactly public or private). The active/
passive distinction (as in active production/passive consumption) is equally problematic. Popular culture involves
choices, reasons, arguments – low theory – even in moments
of consumption, and pleasure industries have more often
responded to emerging organisations of taste then created
them – most recently, for example, in the fad for health and
fitness.

Modleski

High culture critics traditionally put themselves on the
side of the artist – their job is to explain the artist's vision/
work from the artist's point of view (hence the cultural television programmes like the *South Bank Show*); popular culture critics identify with the consumers, ar openly involved
in the struggle for the meaning of goods once they have
reached the market. The resulting politics of pleasure cannot
easily be separated, historically, from the politics of leisure,
from struggles over education, time and space, cultural
capital or from the question of signifying power – who can
make meanings stick? Consider current debates about pornography, 'video nasties', and censorship. What does it mean
when the BBC bans a record like 'Relax'?

It is a recent convention among left-wing cultural com-
mentators, at least in the fields of film and popular music,
to celebrate the works that are seen as most disruptive (punk,
for example). Good art means art which promotes change;
bad art confirms the status quo. Culture is identified with
ideological reproduction; anything which makes such reproduction difficult – the avant-garde! – is dandy. But if it is
capitalism that disrupts people's lives, reorganises their
desires, then popular culture may articulate its most political
class consciousness, its most revolutionary forms in its resistance to change, its statement of 'traditional' human values.
This is to return us to the old-left folk argument but with a
new twist: the question is how the constant cultural need to

look back to hold on, comes to be enmeshed, excitingly, dismayingly, with the drive towards *new* consumption?

I am not going to answer that question here, just use it to signal a plea that writers in popular film and television (and music) should take seriously their own experinces of the texts, their own contradictory positionings – should move, that is, from a high cultural to a popular cultural mode of analysis.

I will begin, then, with the Barry Manilow problem.[2] My question is not why is Manilow so successful, but why does his music have an *emotional* impact when he seems so personally anonymous, so uninteresting in terms of vocal style or arrangement? The first clue to his pop appeal is that he started his career as a commercial jingle writer, but I am sure that the reason for his impact – even the wariest listeners can feel their 'heart strings pulled' – is that he makes the sort of music that these days come at the end of a Hollywood film, writes the sort of song that plays as we leave the cinema and re-arrange our feelings.

Theme songs (rather than soundtrack excerpts) have been an important source of pop hits since the 1950s ('High Noon' is an obvious example, or Henri Mancini numbers like 'Moon River'), and this is clearly an aspect of how Hollywood film music is planned – part of the promotional drama surrounding a new James Bond film, for example, concerns who is going to be chosen to write and sing the theme tune, and in the 1960s traditional film scorers like Bernard Herrmann denounced the degeneration of film music into pop song. But if such songs have a straight commercial object – there is extra money to be made from pop (the American charts, in particular, have been dominated by film themes in recent years)[3] and a well-timed theme record release is an extremely effective film trailer – they have a filmic significance too, particularly given their function of closing a film. Theme songs work, first, as *summary,* they reprise a melody we have been hearing all through the film. Secondly, the songs capture the *mood* of an ending – romantic harmony, new wisdom, social uplift. And thirdly, theme songs often seem to have a built-in sense of sadness or *nostalgia:* the film is over, we have to withdraw from its experience, get 'back to reality'.

What interests me here, though, is not these musical functions as such, but the fact that *songs* are now conventionally used to perform these functions – music, that is, with voices and words neither of which need have anything to do with characters or dialogue in the film (usually, indeed, the only obvious link between a film and its song is the shared title and even that is becoming less common). The effect of this is that the song become a kind of *commentary* on the film: the singers represent us, the audience, and our response to the film, but also become our teachers, making sure we got the film's emotional message.

These songs do this by using pop's own emotional conventions and thus place films in a much wider framework of pop romance and pop common sense. The 1983 norm for such songs, for example, was the male/female duet, which enabled the music both to articularte vocally the male/female basis of Hollywood love and also to stylise emotional intimacy. Hit examples are Joe Cocker's and Jennifer Warnes's 'Up Where We Belong' (from *An Officer and a Gentleman*) and James Ingrams's and Pattie Austin's 'How Do You Keep the Music Playing?' (from *Best Friends*). Both songs draw on black musical techniques of emotional expression (which have nothing to do with the films in question) and both make generalised reference to the future – 'who knows what tomorrow will bring?' 'how do you keep the music playing, how do you make it last?' – which link the mood of the end of the film to the mood of the end of watching the film. (And both songs reveal how useful the synthesiser is in preserving the Hollywood equation of love and the sound of massed strings.)

My conclusion from these example is that we cannot

develop an explanation of how music works in film without reference to an explanation of how popular music works more generally. From this perspective, it is surprising how often in film studies it is asserted, in Schoenberg's words, that 'music never drags a meaning around with it', that it is non-representational, 'abstract art par excellence' (Eisler), 'useless' (Adorno). Such assertions are the basis of numerous accounts of how a film's 'musical system' supports or counters its 'visual system'. My sense of pop music is that, in fact, it drags all sorts of meanings into and out of films. There is a standard musicological exercise, for example, in which people are played pieces of instrumental music and asked to write down their 'associations'. The results (when I gave the paper on which this chapter is based in Birmingham, I played pieces of the soundtracks of *The Big Country, Psycho, A Summer Place* and *American Gigolo*) suggest both that there are widely shared conventions of musical meaning and that these conventions are partly derived from people's shared experiences of film soundtracks.

Claudia Gorbman (who has written the best essay on narrative film music) suggests that we should think in terms of three sorts of musical code: (a) pure musical codes, generating musical discourse, music referring to music itself; (b) cultural musical codes, music referring to the usual cultural context of its production and consumption; and (c) cinematic musical codes, music in formal relationship to co-existent elements in a film.[4]

In practice, though, these different 'levels' are hard to separate. Take the distinction between pure and cultural musical codes. The concept of a pure musical code draws on an account of 'classical' music, on the possibility of a formal, structural analysis of rational, tonal music organised by certain compositional regulations. But this is a peculiar form of music, music without words or direct social function, which is, Eisler suggested, specific to bourgeois culture and has to be understood as such. The 'purity' of the music is, in other words, itself a cultural code and, in fact, music in the classical tradition is heard to express the 'soul' of its composer and to convey or invoke particular sorts of imagery. Both these readings of classical music are important for the continuous use the cinema has made of nineteenth-century romantic music. One early use of film, for example, was to show the images taken to lie in the accompanying music (just like rock videos now). Miklos Rozsa provides an entertaining account of the possible complexity of the inter-pay between musical and film images:

Billy Wilder approached me at a party and said he loved my violin concerto, and that he had worn out his copy of the record and wondered if I had another one. I was as intrigued as much as flattered but all he would say was, 'I've got an idea'. Some months later he called me into his office and revealed the idea: he had written a screenplay called *The Private Life of Sherlock Holmes* and he had written it around my concerto, inspired by the fact that Holmes liked playing the fiddle. The theme of the first movement is somewhat nervous and this apparently suggested to Wilder Holmes' addiction to cocaine. The theme of the second movement of the concerto brought a lady spy to Wilder's mind, and the turbulent third movement conjured up for him the Loch Ness monster. He said, 'This is perfect monster music'. I wasn't flattered but he was right, it did work out quite well. I agreed to score the film for him using the concerto. He seemed to think this would be easy because I wouldn't have to think up any new themes. Actually it was very difficult. The concerto was not written with any images in mind and the timings had to be altered to fit the film sequences. It would have been much easier to invent something fresh.[5]

The most interesting current approach to musical 'mood' conventions is being developed in Sweden by the musicologist Philip Tagg. He cites an experiment performed by one of his Gothenburg colleagues in a postgraduate seminar:

A psychologist from Lund read what a patient had said while listening to a particular piece of music under hypnosis (the instruc-

tions to the patient had been to say what the music made him/her
see, like in a daydream). The seminar knew neither the identity
nor anything else about the piece of music which had given rise
to the patient's associations which were roughly as follows. Alone
out in the countryside on a gently sloping field or meadow near
some trees at the top of the rise where there was the view of a lake
and the forest on the other side. Using this information only, the
seminar was asked to make a rough score of the sort of music they
thought might have evoked such associations. The seminar's sketch
consisted of high notes (perhaps flageolets) sustained in the violins
and a low pedal point in the cellos and basses. These two pitch
polarities were in consonant (either octave or fifth) relations to
each other. A rather undecided, quiet but slightly uneasy figure
was put into the viola part now and again while a solo woodwind
instrument (either flute, oboe or clarinet) played a quasi-modal
legato melodic line which wandered slowly and slightly aimlessly
piano over the rest of the almost static sounds (pianissimo). The
seminar's quick sketch proved to correspond on most counts with
the original musical stimulous which was the taptoe from Vaughan
Williams's *Pastoral Symphony.*[6]

Tagg's own research interest is in the 'mood music collec-
tions' that are used by companies making film commercials,
industrial documentaries, government promotions and a
variety of cinema entertainments. The coding of musical
moods dates back to the ways in which nineteenth-century
music was taken to carry meanings, and Tagg suggests that
there were material reasons why the cinema took over these
'classical' conventions:

there was no technically, economically, socially or culturally viable
music for use in the early years of the capitalist film industry other
then that provided by the bourgeois musical tradition. There was
no other storable music, neither in graphic, mechanical, optical
nor electronic form, neither was there any other sort of transcultur-
ally viable 'nature music' other than that of the bourgeoisie (p. 8).

Tagg's point here is that such 'nature music' is ideologically
loaded; the music represents a particular account of 'nature'.

Today the mood music catalogues cross reference 'nature' themes and sounds with various emotional labels, such that 'nature is mainly viewed as a positive, pleasant source of relaxation and recreation, as a leisure facility, as a backcloth for romance, as a historical-meditative retreat' (p. 24). Similar assumptions lay behind the use of cue sheets in silent film accompaniment, pioneered by Max Winkler, a music publisher's clerk with an exceptional musical memory, whose catalogue 'listed all the compositions under categories – action music, animal music, church music – sinister, chaste, sad, mysterious, majestic, furious etc., etc.'[7] In this context (especially as Winkler later confessed to 'dismembering the great masters. We murdered the works of Beethoven, Mozart, Grieg, J. S. Bach. . .') it is difficult to lay bare 'pure musical codes'. The question becomes how we come to have associations for sounds and structures, how the pure and cultural musical codes relate to each other.

Cultural and cinematic musical codes are similarly entangled, if only because our 'cultural' understanding of musical meanings is, by this stage of cultural history, so dependent on their recurring film contexts. As film composer George Antheil put it in 1945:

Hollywood music is very nearly a public communication, like radio. If you are a movie fan (and who isn't?) you may sit in a movie theatre three times a week listening to the symphonic background scores which Hollywood composers concoct. What happens? Your musical tastes become molded by these scores, heard without knowing it. You *see* love, and you *hear* it. Simultaneously. It makes sense. Music suddenly become a language for you, without your knowing it.[8]

This is to raise a number of historical questions. How, for example, did silent film pianists develop their sense of 'appropriate' accompaniment? How significant were cue sheets? To hear someone play for a silent film today, is to hear someone drawing on the expectations of solo piano (whether

Chopin or Russ Conway) and on implicit assumptions about how silent films *should* sound – the piano now is played to connote the piano then. The interplay of music's cultural and cinematic meanings has its own history (and it would be interesting in this context to compare Hollywood's effect on popular music with the development of popular film and music in India). In cinema's early history, accompanying music was part of the process in which cinema became 're-spectable'; nowadays the absence of music is taken as the sign of a film's seriousness. Music may carry a meaning in film, in short, by drawing attention to the 'cultural conventions of its cinematic use', by drawing on genre rules, for example, which may or may not be confirmed by other aspects of the film.

If popular forms (jazz and country music, rock and roll and disco) first get used in films to signal their 'outside' social source (black culture, southern culture, youth culture, and so on), their use is often soon so stylised as to refer, rather, to their place in previous films. Early 1970s black action films, for example (*Shaft, Superfly, Trouble Man,* etc.), so encoded the 'wah wah' guitar that its use in a film score now (in 1982's *Vortex,* say) inevitably appeals to our ability to draw on *film* references. (Rock has often been taken to be a problematic form for film scorers – its very *presence* can swamp surrounding visual images. Rock videos, though, reveal that rock's musical meanings can soon be closed down by the systematic use of visual clichés.) The most interesting film composers (I am particularly intrigued by Bernard Herrmann and Ennio Morricone) draw on music's ability to cross and *confuse* cinematic and cultural codes in their construction of sound 'narratives'.[9]

One paradox of film music is that while 'high theorists' have paid much less attention to aural than to visual codes, 'ordinary' film viewers (low theorists?) take the complications of musical reference for granted. In the Birmingham weekend (see note 2) discussion of television commercials, for instance, I noted the following casual musical descriptions: 'middle-of-the-road', 'background', 'up-beat', 'Close Encounters climactic', 'new-exciting-world-just-around-the-corner', 'youth music', 'homely, healthy, folky'. Everyone present seemed to understand and agree with such descriptions even though they draw on a remarkable jumble of references and assumption, and fuse musical, cultural, historical and cinematic allusions. I want to keep this in mind in addressing the three issues that have most fruitfully occupied more systematic approaches to film music.

Realism

In common-sense terms it might seem that music is the 'non-realist' aspect of films, yet audiences take it for granted that strings accompany a clinch. Indeed, a clinch without strings may seem *less* real, though another film convention is to climax a sex scene with silence, as if to register its 'privacy' (and our voyeuristic embarrassment). The point of this example is to stress that music is as essential to the perceived 'truth' of a film as everything else, but the reality music describes/refers to is a different sort of reality than that described/referred to by visual images. Film composers themselves often take their cue on this from Wagner, who argued that the purpose of music was 'to amplify what can't be shown' – and what cannot be shown is regularly called 'atmosphere' or 'mood'. Broadly speaking, two strands of reality seem to be involved here: First, *emotional reality*. Music, it seems can convey and clarify the emotional significance of a scene, the true 'real' feelings of the characters involved in it. Music, in short, reveals what is 'underneath' or 'behind' a film's observable gestures. Thus, for composer Jerry Goldsmith, the aim of film music is 'emotional penetration', while in Elmer Bernstein's words:

The job of the composer is really very varied. You must use your art to heighten the emotional aspects of the film – music can tell the story in purely emotional terms and the film by itself cannot. The reason that it can't is that it's a visual language and basically intellectual. You look at an image and you then have to interpret what it means, whereas if you listen to something or someone and you understand what you hear – that's an emotional process. Music is particularly emotional – if you are affected by it, you don't have to ask what it means.[10]

Secondly, *reality of time and place*. Another recurring point made by the film scorers interviewed by Tony Thomas is how much research they do. In writing music for a film set in a particular historical period or in a particular geographical place, they must produce sounds which current audiences believe relate to what people in that time or place would have 'really' heard. This is a more complicated matter than it might seem. The 'reality' of film musical settings actually refers to historical and geographical myths (themselves constructed, in part, by previous music in previous films set in these places and times). Thus the music for *Zorba the Greek* became so powerfully connotative of Greece that Greek restaurants (even those in Greece itself) have to use the music to convince customers of their 'Greekness'. And a time and a place can have an emotional meaning too (this is one of the functions of 'nature music'). The Australian *Picnic at Hanging Rock* thus conveyed the 'mystery' of the rock by using Gheorghe Zamfir's eastern European pan pipes (underscored by a cathedral organ), while Michael Nyman's score for *The Draughtsman's Contract* used the appropriate historical musical form but scored instrumentally according to the rules of contemporary minimalism, thus making the apparent celebration of 'order' distinctly unsettling.

All these examples of musical realism raise the question of how audiences *recognise* musical authenticity. It is easy to move (like Elmer Bernstein) from the directness of music's emotional impact to an assertion of its 'natural' meaning, so it is worth citing another cautionary musicological story: a group of African musicians, invited to tour the US folk festival circuit, found that their music was getting a decidedly cool response, was being dismissed as 'commercial'. After a few weeks the musicians sat down and worked out a new arrangement of their material, designed specifically to signal 'authenticity' in American folk terms. With this 'fake' sound (it bore little relationship to the music they played in their home country) they became widely praised for their 'ethnic' flair. More recently, Jeremy Marre's series of films for Channel Four on popular music in Asia was criticised by critics because, in the words of the *Sunday Times* (18 March 1984) it didn't include 'enough indigenous melody as opposed to processed western pop'. Marre's point, of course, was to show that this distinction is nowadays meaningless.

Diagesis

The most systematic theoretical approach to film music begins by distinguishing its diagetic use (when it has a place in 'the narratively implied spatio-temporal world of the actions and characters', when it is made by the band in a night-club scene, for exmple) and its non-diagetic use (when the music heard has no source within the film's own world). The important point here, as Claudia Gorbman has made clear, is that in pratice music straddles this apparently clear divide. How, for example, do we classify the moment when someone remembers a tune and we hear it on the soundtrack – the physical production of the music is non-diagetic, but its emotional production is diagetic. Is the character 'really hearing something'?

More generally, it seems that our classification of music in terms of diagesis depends on an implicit sense of sounds' *appropriateness* to a scene, in terms, that is, of musical realism (which, as I have already suggested, is not the same thing as visual realism). If, for example, the diagetic/non-diagetic distinction refers to the source of a sound, then this is not just a question of what we can actually see in a scene but of what we might *expect to see* as part of the film's realistic 'sound-scape'. In *The Godfather*, for example, Nino Rota's score uses and makes deliberate reference to Italian street music, to 'live' sounds, even when the musicians could not possibly be present in the narrative. This is a non-diagetic use of music, but one which is drawing our attention to the music's previous 'real' presence. In youth films from *American Graffiti* to *The Big Chill*, to give a different sort of example, rock and roll is so much part of the 'diagesis' (and we do indeed see radios and record-players turned on, even records being played by Wolfman Jack himself) that it is misleading to assert that in those scenes when such music has no 'real' source that it suddenly becomes non-diagetic. Disco music is used similarly in *Saturday Night Fever:* in the love scene, 'How Deep Is Your Love' is the sort of song that *could* have been on the radio or record-player – the implication is that the film characters are 'hearing' it as clearly as we are in the audience. By the time we get to a film like *Blade Runner* we find that the 'reality' of this future Los Angeles is guaranteed precisely by the invisibility of the ever-present synthesised sounds – outside the cinema too we are increasingly surrounded by music which has no apparent source.[11]

Subjectivity

The third important question raised by theoretical debate is how music works to position film spectators (or auditors), and this is to address the question of emotional realism from a slightly different perspective: one function of film music is to reveal our emotions as the *audience*. Film music is often said to have physical effects – sending shivers down the spine, bringing a lump to the throat – and sounds, more obviously than visions, have collective effects – we hear a beat and tap our feet (or march or work) together. Film scores are thus important in representing *community* (via martial or nationalistic music, for example) in both film and audience. The important point here is that as spectators we are drawn to identify not with the film characters themselves but with their emotions, which are signalled pre-eminently by music which can offer us emotional experience *directly*. Music is central to the way in which the pleasure of cinema is simultaneously individualised and shared; like political rhetoric it can cue responses through the application of general rules of crowd arousal to particular circumstances.

There is, in this context, another sort of approach to musical meaning – the Barthian analysis of music as a *sensuous* pleasure, in which we are overwhelmed by sound (as in *Blade Runner*?). Barthes himself raised the question of why certain sorts of voice give pleasure (speaking as well as singing voices), why we take delight in the experience of meaning *being made*. This is to widen the question of film music in two directions – first by linking it to non-musical but human sounds; secondly by referring us to films, musicals, which are explicitly about music making. In the long run any analysis of music in film will have to cover all this ground, but in this chapter I have been specifically concerned with music's coded pleasures and so my closing questions is this: where do emotional codes come from? This is to go back to the issue of the clinch and the strings: to have meaning, emotions must be shaped, and this is as much a public as a private process, one in which music (and music making) seems central. Do people 'hear harmonies' when they kiss outside films too? To develop the theory of film music we need, in Antoine Hennion's words, 'not so much a sociology of music as a musicology of society'.[12]

Notes

1 Zofia Lissa, *Asthetik der Filmmusik* (Berlin: Henschelvelg, 1965).

2 What follows was first presented as a talk at the SEFT Sound Cinema weekend, Triangle Arts Centre, Birmingham, 29-30 October 1983 and appeared in a slightly different form in *Screen* 25, 1984. Thanks to Philip Tagg for his help.

3 In Britain, by contrast, television themes are more likely to have chart success – like the themes from *Minder, Hill Street Blues* and *Auf Wiedersehen Pet,* or more bizarrely, the arrangement of Ravel's *Bolero* used by Torvill and Dean in their skating triumphs.

4 Claudia Gorbman, 'Narrative film music', *Yale French Studies* 60, 1980, p. 185.

5 Quoted in Tony Thomas, *Music for the Movies* (New York: A. S. Barnes, 1973), pp. 96-7.

6 Philip Tagg, *'Nature' as a Musical Mood Category* (Gothenburg: IASMP, 1983), p. 31.

7 Thomas, *op. cit.,* p. 38.

8 Quoted in Thomas, *op. cit.,* p. 171.

9 For a fuller discussion of this point see Simon Frith, 'Sound and Vision', *Collusion* 1, 1981, pp. 7-9.

10 Quoted in Thomas, *op. cit.,* p. 193.

11 *Blade Runner* has an interesting score for other reasons. Its composer, Vangelis, refused to allow the release of his electronic performance and so it was reproduced, remarkably accurately, by the strings of The New American Orchesta.

12 Antoine Hennion, 'Music as social production', in David Horn and Philip Tagg eds., *Popular Music Perspectives* (Gothenburg and Exeter: IASMP, 1982), p. 40.

The popularity of filmgoing in the US, 1930-50

Film history after film history tell us that 1930 to 1950 represented the stable 'Golden Age' of filmgoing in the US, sandwiched between the 'chaos' of the coming of sound, and the 'new' wide-screen colour images of the 1950s. The constancy of this 'Golden Age' is crucial because it has freed historians to concentrate solely on 'reading' films after quickly brushing over the required socio-economic facts. While it is certainly true that filmgoing in the US reached its apex during the 1930s and 1940s, popularity should not be equated with the lack of change. I think we must first re-examine what the filmgoing experience was during Hollywood's 'Golden Age' before we can make sense of questions about the relative popularity of the cinema.

In this chapter I shall argue that there were at least three significant transformations in the exhibition of cinema in the US during the 1930s and 1940s. Filmgoing remained consistently popular in part because exhibitors were willing to change.

During the first three years of the Great Depression in the US (1930-33), approximately one-third of the movie audience deserted this particular entertainment activity. People worked more and indulged in less costly entertainments. Exhibitors reacted slowly. For some twenty years they had seen audiences steadily increase, unaffected by earlier recessions. However, in 1931, theatre owners began to cut costs.

First to go were the services which had been so common in movie palace entertainment during the 1920s. The movie palaces of the 1920s had utilised doormen, ushers, and even nurses to help with child-care. Although ushers never fully disappeared, their role switched from crowd assistance to crowd control. High school students (15-18 years old), receiving the minimum wage, replaced more expensive university students as ushers. Several chains even recruited women, for cost-cutting and sexist reasons. Consider the following recommendation made in a manual for theatre managers: 'In (theatres) where carpets, draperies, and furnishings are worn, and some of the luster has faded, beautiful young usherettes, attractively costumed, help keep the public's eye off the shabby spots. In small operations, usherettes can also save the management the expense of a maid'.[1]

But cutting costs, as is discovered over and over again during the early phases of recessions, never truly solves the problem. By 1932 exhibitors in the US had done as much as they could on the cost side. They needed to increase revenues or go out of business (many did go out of business). Quickly they innovated the first transformation: double features, two features for the price of one. This was not a new idea; most historians of the cinema place its origination in or about 1915. During the 1920s, only a handful of small neighbourhood theatre owners, unable to obtain attractive films from the major companies, resorted to double features. US filmgoers more typically saw one feature, a couple of shorts, a newsreel, and possibly a stage show for their entrance fee of fifteen to seventy-five cents (about seventy-five cents to $4.25 in present dollar figures).

During the early 1930s many exhibitors, whether affiliated with the major corporations or not, turned to double features. An equal number also instituted games and lotteries to attract customers. However, in 1933, the US federal government through the National Recovery Act outlawed all giveaways and games as 'unfair competition'. With these forms of lure unavailable, nearly all US theatres turned to double features.[2]

The widespread adoption of what were then known in the trade as 'duals' resulted in a new formula for movie shows. A complete show became longer and longer, and so a theatre would 'turn over' fewer times each day. Initially this loss of potential income was overcome by increased attendance. For example, there might be four instead of five shows a day, but if attendance per show would rise by thirty per cent, the theatre owner would come out ahead. But, as more and more theatres began to 'double', any single theatre's relative advantage lessened. Thus, during the mid to late 1930s, there was continual debate concerning the merits of abandoning double features, but such action never came about.[3]

Initially public opinion (as expressed through random sample surveys) was decidedly against double features, despite the fact that millions attended them each day. For example, a poll taken in 1937 by *Fortune*, a highly respected business magazine, reported that only one-fifth of those surveyed would attend a double feature when given the opportunity to go to a single feature. The tradition of the single feature, a fixture of filmgoing in the US for nearly a generation, would not pass away easily. Opponents provided three objections to double features: (1) Their excessive length caused eye strain and fatigue; (2) 'good' films were too often paired with 'poor' films; and (3) fewer quality shorts subjects were being presented.

For a time laws were proposed banning or restricting double features. This political controversy came to a head in 1938 in Chicago. Since this city had one of the strongest traditions of stage shows accompanying films, Paramount, the dominant theatre chain, had long resisted completely switching to double features. But, with profits declining, in 1938 Paramount instituted double features throughout the second largest city in the US. There was a public outcry; 200 members of the local Parent Teachers Association marched on City Hall. Independent exhibitors appealed to the Chicago City Council to pass a law restricting double features. Health hazards to children were the reasons opponents cited when pressing for the new law.

But Paramount represented a powerful corporate presence in Chicago, and was able to get the City Council to table the issue. Thwarted by city politics, opponents turned to the state legislature of Illinois. Rural exhibitors co-operated with the owners of small neighbourhood houses from Chicago and this coalition pushed a bill restricting double features through the General Assembly of Illinois. The proposed law would have limited all film shows in the state of Illinois to two hours and fifteen minutes, thus outlawing all double features save serials or non-competitive 'B' films from small studios such as Republic and Monogram. Fines and prison sentences were established. But before this measure could become law, the governor of Illinois had to sign it. He refused, and there the matter stalled. Exhibitor groups and parties interested in the safety of children took note; the double feature had become a permanent part of the film exhibition landscape.[4]

Throughout the 1930s exhibitors sought non-filmic ways to attract patrons to their double features. One practice which clearly differentiated a theatre's product was air-conditioning. After the First World War the US film industry had significantly pushed along the innovation and diffusion of climate control. Before 1917 US theatres of all types had employed extensive fan systems or simply closed their doors during the summer months. But during the first two decades of the twentieth century, inventors learned how to create appliances to cool and then dehumidify and cool, large spaces. By 1925 air-conditioned theatres, especially those in Chicago, were the talk of the film industry. The sole problem was that the systems were so large and so expensive that only picture-palaces of 2,000 or more seats could afford installation.[5]

All this changed during the Great Depression. During the early 1930s the Carrier Corporation introduced a compact, relatively cheap air-conditioning system costing about $10,000 (about $50,000 in 1984 dollars) for a 500 seat neighbourhood theatre, and about $25,000 (about $125,000 in 1984 dollars) for a 1,000 seat theatre. The Chicago World's Fair of 1933-4 served to publicise air-conditioning technology, but in the depressed times of the 1930s the new Carrier units were principally installed for the convenience of the rich in luxury Pullman cars, fancy hotels, expensive restaurants, and large homes. Film theatres were one of the few public institutions where the middle-class and poor citizens of the US could indulge in cool, dehumidified comfort until well into the 1950s.[6]

During the 1930s owners of film theatres throughout the US, especially in the south and west, installed air-conditioning, pushing sales of air-conditioning equipment to a record fifty million dollars in 1936. While the economy of the US turned down again in 1937, sales of air-conditioning equipment continued to boom, reaching one hundred million dollars in 1941. Expansion came to an abrupt halt with the US entry into the Second World War. But the war prompted even greater development of air-conditioning technology as the US government pushed to increase productivity in crowded factories, especially shipbuilding plants.

Air-conditioning sales to US film theatres commenced again as soon as the US left its war-time economy. By 1950, while few homes in the US had air-conditioning, more than three-quarters of all movie houses had installed a system. This comparative advantage held throughout the 1950s, and only in 1960s and 1970s America have we seen the rise of total air-conditioned cultures in the 'Sun-belt'. (The Texas cities of Dallas and Houston could hardly exist in their present form without air-conditioned buildings.) We should not underestimate how important the comparative advantage of air-conditioning was to film exhibition in the US during the 1930s and 1940s. Going to see a film in that era became a year-round treat.[7] Indoor entertainment could provide welcome relief from the heat and humidity whether either of the feature films was entertaining or not.[8]

Double features and air-conditioning enabled movie exhibitors to offer a different product. Once on firmer footing by the mid-1930s, exhibitors began to look to expand the base of their revenue production. They wanted to make profit creation less dependent on the popularity of the feature films. Thus, they internalised the sales of a complementary good which had long been associated with going to the movies, the eating of sweets and popcorn and the consumption of soft drinks.

During the first three decades of filmgoing in the US patrons purchased their treats before or after the show from a nearby shop. Pictures of cinemas taken during the 1920s invariably display an adjacent confectionery store. During the 1920s more and more small neighbourhood theatres sold sweets. At that time auditoria were kept dark, and ushers led patrons to their seat. Pre-packaged confectionery could be easily handled, required little investment, and dictated little alteration in the theatre lobby. Still, few picture palaces bothered. The added revenue was not needed, and the sales of sweets in a theatre had too long been associated with 'low class' burlesque shows.

The decline in profits associated with the Great Depression changed the minds of theatre owners. They had already fired a majority of their ushers, turned up the auditorium lights, and let patrons move freely about the theatre. Patrons only needed to be encouraged to move to the refreshment stand. By the mid-1930s nearly all theatres had confectionery counters in place. The necessary investment was small, and the added revenues often provided the difference between a profit and loss. By 1936 sales of confectionery in US movie houses topped ten million dollars, contributing some five million to the pockets of theatre owners.[9]

Then came popcorn. For decades vendors had sold this snack food to film patrons from wagons positioned outside theatres. Theatre owners simply moved the popcorn stand into the lobby. It was easy to manufacture, and its aroma could entice waiting customers. But best of all, popcorn was one food which Americans increased (not decreased) their consumption of during the bad economic times. With popcorn, because it is so relatively cheap, sales go up as incomes go down because people substitute it for other more costly treats.

During the late 1930s exhibitors popped corn by the train-car load. The theatres associated with the largest chains, those owned by the major Hollywood movie corporations, took advantage of cost savings by negotiating for corn purchase in bulk. Consequently they could produce a fifteen cent box for three cents. Even with the other associated costs, (wages to salespersons, containers and popping apparatus) profit rates more often than not exceeded 100 per cent.

The film industry pushed popcorn into the status of an important US farm crop. The US popcorn harvest grew from five million pounds in 1934 to more than one hundred million pounds in 1940. During the Second World War popcorn became a fixture at theatres. And production of popcorn during the war, with much land devoted to growing food for troops, still soared beyond four hundred million pounds per year. That represented more than four pounds of popcorn for every person in the US.[10]

The third phase in the introduction of the sale of food in the cinema came after the Second World War as other snack food companies expanded into the film theatre market. The Coca-Cola corporation led the way. In conjunction with Morton's salt (on popcorn to create thirst) Coke pushed to have theatre owners create virtual confectionery super-markets in the lobbies of their theatres. It was then that theatre owners ritualised the intermission in order to provide two chances to sell snack foods to a captured audience. To many theatre owners films became secondary to the sales of food. The feature film and air-conditioned environment may have pulled patrons into the theatre, but it was from the sales of popcorn, Coca-Cola, and confectionery that the exhibitors made their profits.

This intervention has sought to demonstrate that the cinema exhibition in the US did not remain constant during the 1930s and 1940s. Double features, air-conditioning, and confectionery sales significantly altered the way Americans experienced filmgoing. Popularity of the movies *per se never* assured consistent profits. (Even today we can not concentrate too long on the popularity of the cinema, for exhibitors look to snack food sales to produce the bulk of their profits.)

Thus in the end we return to the question: what is filmgoing? Long ignored, this seemingly simple question turns out, I would argue, to stand as the key issue when exploring the relative popularity of film versus other mass entertainments. It is very difficult to learn the precise nature of filmgoing in the US because at least in the US there have been few instances when films stood alone as the economic draw. During the history of the commercial cinema in the US feature films rarely have been able to stand alone as a source of profit. Thus we need to allocate further study to the changing nature of the entertainment package offered by exhibitors. The history of filmgoing is one of constant change, and those of us who study the cinema have much to learn about the nature of these socio-economic (and psychological) transformations.

Notes

1 Frank H. Ricketson, Jr., *The Management of Motion Picture Theatres* (New York: McGraw-Hill, 1938), p. 126.

2 For more on the relations of the National Recovery Act and the US film industry see Douglas Gomery, 'Hollywood, the national recovery administration, and the question of monopoly power', in Gorham A. Kindem, ed, *The American Movie Industry* (Carbondale: Southern Illinois University Press, 1982), pp. 205-14.

3 Robert W. Chambers, 'The double feature as a sales problem', *Harvard*

Business Review, 16, 2, winter, 1938, pp. 226-36; 'Spreading of double feature alarms leaders of industry', *Motion Picture Herald*, 14 November 1931, p. 9; and 'Most section turning on doubles', *Motion Picture Herald*, 8 July 1933, p. 9.

4 Brad Angier, 'Duals now a Frankenstein in their New England cradle', *Motion Picture Herald*, 2 November 1935, p. 42; 'Double movie scrap', *Business Week*, 5 March 1938, pp 45-6; 'Civic groups join in legislation move on double bills in Chicago', *Motion Picture Herald*, 19 February 1938, p. 23; 'Balaban reports dual bills gaining', *Motion Picture Herald*, 25 June 1938, p. 41; and 'Illinois governor declares bill banning duals unconstitutional', *Motion Picture Herald*, 5 August 1939, p. 28.

5 R. E. Cherne, 'Developments in refrigeration as applied to air conditioning', *Ice and Refrigeration*, CI, 1941, pp. 29-30; and Oscar E. Anderson, *Refrigeration in America* (Princeton: Princeton University Press, 1953), pp. 309-11.

6 Margaret Ingels, *Willis Haviland Carrier: Father of Air Conditioning* (New York: Doubleday and Co., 1952), *passim;* Carl F. Boester, 'New things in air conditioning that are bringing lower costs', *Motion Picture Herald – Better Theatres*, 18 March 1939, pp. 6-7; and John Eberson, 'Theatre construction costs today', *Motion Picture Herald – Better Theatres*, 15 October 1938, pp. 9-11.

7 Of course today the US film industry extracts the bulk of its revenues and profits from screening during the summer months. The film industry takes air conditioning for granted. But without it current rates of profitability would be impossible.

8 J. H. Toler, 'Air conditioning wanted for new and remodeled theatres', *Domestic Engineering* 165, March 1945, pp. 113-14; and 'Air conditioning: biggest year yet', *Business Week*, 27 June 1953, pp. 43-4, 46.

9 'Candy holds its appeal among patrons of theatres', *Motion Picture Herald – Better Theatres,* 22 March 1952, pp. 55-7; and 'What's playing at the Grove?', *Fortune* 38, August 1948, pp. 94-6.

10 Charles E. Buckhead, *Rice, Popcorn and Buckwheat by States, 1866-1953,* Statistical Bulletin 238, United States Department of Agriculture (Washington DC: USGPO, 1958), pp. 10-17; 'Popcorn crazy', *Saturday Evening Post* 221, 21 May 1949, pp. 36, 141; 'Now it's popcorn: latest wartime shortage', *Business Week*, 17 June 1944, p. 66; and John J. Riley, *A History of the American Soft Drink Industry, 1807-1957*, (Washington: American Bottlers of Carbonated Beverages, 1958), pp. 142-52.

Melodrama
in and out of the home

In the 1950s, the Hollywood studio system was faced with three massive crises: the impact of the HUAC (House of UnAmerican Activities Committee) investigation, indictment as a monopoly under the anti-trust laws, and the coming of television. The first two provided an ideological and economic background to the third, which broke the genealogical links connecting different forms of popular theatrical entertainment that stretched back to the early days of urban industrialised culture. Television revolutionised the conditions of spectatorship associated with mass entertainment. Mass urban cultures of spectacle had always assumed a communal audience, collected together in larger or smaller spaces, from the vast theatres of the London melodrama, the Keith Vaudeville Bijou in Boston or the small shop-front nickelodeons of early cinema. The cinema's birth as a mass art can be fixed at the moment when the Kinetoscope gave way to communal theatrical viewing.[1] Television broke up this audience, to create a home-based mode of consumption that was prefigured by radio but without precedent as mass visual entertainment. Whereas the appeal of films was posited on 'going out', television appeals to 'staying in'. The draw of the city lights at night, the neon, the names of the stars, the glamour of the Palaces, was at an end.

The success of television as a means of mass entertainment was historically secondary to its success as a consumer

durable. The 1950s saw a swing to domesticity that complemented the US economy's expansion in production. And
then, as *Rosie the Riveter* has evoked so vividly, American
women were being tempted and dragooned back into the
home to readjust the unsettling effects of the Second World
War on the division of labour between the sexes. Conservative retrenchment, epitomised by McCarthy, was reinforced
by the war in Korea and confidence in the dollar, the post-war
international currency. In Douglas Sirk's words 'America was
feeling safe and sure of herself, a society primarily sheltering
its comfortable achievements and institutions'.[2] Hollywood
acknowledged the nature of the crisis by resorting desperately
to technical innovations and gimmicks to lure audiences away
from the television and out of the home. It is perhaps no
accident that the fifties are marked by the particular
resurgence of the family melodrama, the Hollywood genre
associated with the dramas of domesticity, woman, love and
sexuality. While fifties Hollywood put a brave and colourful
face on its difficulties, filling the wide screen with Western
landscapes and spectacular casts of thousands, the melodrama
drew its source material from unease and contradiction
within the very icon of American life, the home, and its
sacred figure, the mother.

For me, the melodrama is represented first and foremost
by Douglas Sirk and the movies he made during the 1950s.
The last phase of his Hollywood career captures the pivotal
spirit of the decade and the melodrama's own aesthetic
pleasure in coincidence. He signed a contract with Universal
studios in 1950 and left the US for ever in 1959. In 1955 he
directed *All That Heaven Allows*. In the movie's central scene,
Jane Wyman, playing a widow in her forties, is given a television set by her grown-up children. This Christmas gift
celebrates her decision to stay and live in their old family
home, renouncing her sexuality and reaffirming the pro-
perty-based values of her bourgeois milieu. The television
set becomes charged with metaphor and connotation linking

middle-class interior, motherhood, prosperity and re-pression. But the formal staging of the scene, its dramatic construction, evokes something more: the fact that television sprang, Minerva-like, fully grown into the American home, into the midst of the American family, the source material of the Hollywood melodrama itself. It is as though, at the moment of defeat, Hollywood could afford to point out the seeds of decay in its victrious rival's own chosen breeding ground.

How things end can throw previous experience into unex-pected perspectives. The home, as a social place and mythologised space, has a special significance for the new medium, and can thus draw attention to the way that oppos-itions of inside/outside have given order and pattern to the centrifugal/centripetal tensions in urban, industrialised, capitalist life. This imagery of place and space can, perhaps, link the complex strands interconnecting the class and sexual politics of popular entertainment. The worker, often immi-grant, the raw material of the labour force, is culturally marginalised, often literally displaced. Spheres of male or female space closely define economic and social expressions of sexual difference. Popular entertainment has been increas-ingly absorbed by and drawn into an ordered national con-sensus (in which the 'home' performs a particular, icon-like role) but its origins lay on the margins of society within the very first urban, industrialised proletariat. And the spectacles of the early nineteenth-century melodrama were the first means of expression for this new class, in a new social and economic order.

Economics

A jump from the Hollywood melodrama of the 1950s to the early nineteenth-century melodrama brackets a particular strand in popular culture, from its birth in the crowded city streets to its death in the television dominated home. But the chaotic crowds in the streets and the contained privacy of the home both have their origins in an urban industrialised environment, and are bound together as each other's other side of the coin. The family audience, under the aegis of the mother, constituted a rhetorical excuse and means towards broadening, step by step, the appeal of popular theatrical entertainment out of the margins into the sphere of respectability, and simultaneously placing it on a firm capitalist and entrepreneurial basis.

In a remarkable chapter on Coney Island, in his book *Delirious New York,* Rem Koolhaas analyses three stages in the cultural and economic development of the amusement park that provides a suggestive paradigm for the more complex and extended transitions in popular theatrical entertainment:

The triad of personalities and professions that Tilyou, Thompson and Reynolds represent – amusement expert/professional architect/ developer politician – is reflected in the character of the three parks: *Steeplechase,* where the park format is invented almost by accident under the hysterical demand for entertainment; *Luna,* where the format is invested with thematic and architectural coherence; and finally *Dreamland* where the preceeding breakthroughs are elevated to an ideological plane by a professional politician.

Reynolds realises that to succeed, Dreamland must transcend its compromised origins and become a post-proletarian park 'the first time in the history of Coney Island Amusement that an effort has been made to provide a place of amusement that appeals to all classes'.[3]

Clearly, there are no exact parallels (Boucicault probably outshines Thompson, while Reynolds' perverse, deviant, carnivalesque Dreamland could not have survived in the Hays dominated world of the film moguls) but the phasing suggests similar patterns of development in other entertainment media.

The first, spontaneous phase evokes the early phases of

the British working-class melodrama, the immigrant vaudeville in the US and the nickelodeon days of the cinema. Here, profits are limited by small-scale investment and the audience restricted to a sizeable but ideologically marginalised sector of the population. The early British melodrama celebrated transitional, liminal themes that included memories of feudal oppression with reflection on the lot of the working man. The world of everyday normality would be turned upside down as the innocent oppressed suffered at the mercy of the dominant, with arbitrary turns of plot and fate reflecting the arbitrary, relentless nature of class justice. There was a direct appeal to the concerns and preoccupations of a recently urbanised working class. By mid-century the social themes of the melodrama went into abeyance as the repeal of the Licensing Act in 1843 brought an end to the legal formal class distinction in British culture (as will be discussed below). This transition was marked by the great rebuilding of the London melodrama theatres in the 1850s, directing the poorer and less respectable towards the developing music-halls until they, in turn, acquired Palace status in the 1880s.

In the early vaudeville, unlike the melodrama, language was central and foregrounded with comic monologues, jokes and sketches that reflected the immigrant audience's own fascination and difficulty with the English language. Ethnicity and difference could be kept alive while a communal celebration of the new society provided a coherence that alleviated the trauma of immigration and urbanisation: . . . 'the slang of the cities, the rough coinage of the labouring classes, the pidgin English of the European immigrants, back-country archaisms and provincial dialects. It is also the language of unarticulated emotions and uncommunicable ideas'.[4]

This entertainment belonged to a no-man's land, in between two worlds, neither one nor the other and both at once. This phase belongs to the experience of marginality and a transition itself suspended between memory and loss on the one hand and aspirations to something new. Once the demands of industrial production and the experience of urban living are internalised, the spectacle offered by popular entertainment changes its significance. It keeps alive the values of the new life, so that they still seem to be within reach, and celebrates wealth, social mobility, success and the machine age. The new world, now accepted but still so far away, exists as the 'other world' of glitter, stars and glamour. Similar in some ways to the early British melodrama, this phase should not be seen as a lost 'Golden Age' of working-class culture but a moment of elongated transition in which heightened awareness and political self-consciousness characterise a position on the margins of society, looking in, rather than being. Albert McLean describes the changed mood of the later vaudeville:

The fantasy ran on according to the laws of its own being, inviting the spectator to identify but not to participate, leaving him at the close with the sense of some inchoate dream, the order and meaning of which lay buried beneath the threshold of consciousness. The dream might be repeated but it was not to be dissected or under-stood.[5]

From the 1850s, the British melodrama rose above its specifically working-class audience and acquired an equivalently higher level of capitalisaton. In 1852 *The Corsican Brothers* was presented in London, pioneering a new emphasis on spectacle and special effects. Spectacular productions demanded investment that went hand in hand with the investment in the spectacular buildings themselves. The amazing illusions of the mid-century gave way later to equally grandiose and expensive enactments of natural reality. This emphasis on appearance finds an echo in Koolhaas's dercription of the architect Thompson's Luna Park development at Coney Island:

Thompson had designed the appearance, the exterior of a magic city. But . . . he is finally unable or unwilling to use his private realm, with all its metaphorical potential, for the design of culture. He is still an architectural Frankenstein whose talent for creating the new far exceeds his ability to control its contents.

Luna's astronauts may be stranded on another planet, in a magic city, but they discover in the sky-scraper forest the over-familiar instruments of pleasure – the Bunny Hug, the Burros, the Circus, the German Village, the Fall of Port Arthur, the Gates of Hell, the Great Train Robbery, the Whirl-the-Whirl.

Luna Park suffers from the self-defeating laws that govern entertainment: it can only skirt the surface of myth, only hint at the anxieties accumulated in the collective unconscious.[6]

When the cinema grew out of the nickelodeons into the age of features and picture palaces, with equivalent increases in finance, nearly a century's development in popular theatrical spectacle existed as a tradition and a frame of reference. The move towards a more monied audience had already produced the great spectacular melodramas of the late nineteenth century and the respectable vaudeville of, for instance, B. F. Keith. Naturally the presence of this popular cultural tradition contributed to the complexity and variety of the cinema but it also acted as a break, a pressure towards conservatism. When D. W. Griffith emerged as the major 'stage manager' of the cinema's shift into the formal and thematic aesthetics and conventions of the big picture, he looked back beyond the comedy and fantasy of the primitive one-reelers to the great theatrical productions of the late melodrama. In doing so he brought a conscious political stance that was already conservative and nostalgic to bear on a dramatic form that had already, itself, been refined into spectacle and sentiment. There seems, in Griffiths's work, to be a desperate refusal to acknowledge the modernity of the cinema, the contemporary world and its aesthetics and, particularly, a new and changing concept of womanhood. It is as though the consolidation and coming of age for this new form of popular entertainment could only take place under the aegis of an exaggerated emphasis on tradition. In this light it seems appropriate that the cinema's first great director should have grown up in a south that was already steeped in the process of creating a nostalgic myth for the *ante-bellum* period, generating an image of the lost 'feudal' south that became standard fare from the Broadway musicals of the 1890s to Griffiths's own contribution, *Birth of a Nation*. Although Eisenstein pays tribute to the energy and modernity of Griffiths's montage, he traces even this innovation back to a nineteenth-century influence, to Dickens.

The theatrical tradition of popular culture constructs its 'post proletarian phase' around a process which dovetails money and morals. In the vaudeville this had involved banning liquor 'to encourage ladies to attend', raising the level of decency in the acts and respectability of the surroundings. 'Christy's Ministrels, Barnum and Pastor all represented attempts to capture the mass audience, and all acknowledged that the secret lay in providing a family entertainment acceptable to the middle class that would also appeal to a general audience.'[7]

B. F. Keith, the greatest of all the vaudeville entrepreneurs, precursor of the film moguls, censored his acts not only from the point of view of decency but also ethnicity, so the moment of transition from immigrant to family audience is marked not only by the presence of ladies, but also of the nation. The audience was now taken to be sufficiently integrated to react to an ethnic joke with laughter at, rather than laughter with. Once again this tradition provided a model for the cinema:

Most important, when (film) exhibitors imagined the new audience, they usually thought of the vaudeville audience – a cross section of urban and sub-urban American life. They preferred this audience to the new, unfashionable audience that had discovered them . . . the problem was, how to lure that affluent family audience, so near and yet so far. The answer was through the New American Woman and her children . . . In a trade hungry for respectability, the middle class woman was respectability incarnate. Her very presence in the theatre refuted vituperative accusations lodged against the common show's corrupting vulgarity.[8]

Architectural changes are one means of marking moments of transition in the economics of popular entertainment. The 'palace' signifies a new level of investment; it also invites a new audience able to pay for quality entertainment. All the great forms of popular theatrical entertainment seem to be affected by this 'drift up', to be then replaced at the lower social level by another type of spectacle. In each case, respect-ability attracts the general audience, and the presence of wife and mother seals the change. It is as though this self-con-scious new grouping, constituted, pampered, even imagined, by entrepreneurs, is the sign that a form of entertainment that was previously on the margins of society has arrived on the 'inside', within the national consensus.

Mythologies

'To jump from the Hollywood melodrama of the 1950s to the early nineteenth-century melodrama brackets a particular strand of popular culture from its birth in the crowded city streets to its death in the television dominated home. But the chaotic crowds in the street and the contained privacy of the home both have their origins in the same urban indus-trialised environment, and are bound together as each other's other side of the coin'. The Manichaean aspect of nineteenth-century culture flourished on oppositions, in Peter Brooks's apt phrase 'the logic of the excluded middle'. Problems of class difference and sexual difference are translated into mythology through a series of spatial metaphors: interior/exterior, inside/outside, included/excluded. The oppositions exist on the level of fear and reassurance, and give an order to the contradictions that haunted the cities of industrialised society.

Under Louis Philippe the private citizen was born . . . For the private citizen, for the first time the living space became distinguished from the place of work. The former constituted itself as the interior. The office was its complement. The private citizen who in the office took reality into account, required of the interior that it support him in his illusions. The necessity was all the more pressing since he had no intention of adding social preoccupations to his business ones. From this sprang the phantasmagorias of the interior.[9]

The separation of public and private spheres within the bourgeoisie gave order to the new experience of industrialised city life and the pressures of production, while also establishing the domestic as the area for consumption. Advertising would soon make use of the 'phantasmagorias of the interior'. But the neat public/private antinomy concealed tensions and contradictions on both sides of its opposition. Benjamin does not mention the fact that the private sphere, the domestic, is an essential adjunct to bourgeoise marriage and is thus associated with woman, not simply as female, but as wife and mother. It is the mother who guarantees the privacy of the home by maintaining its respectability, as essentially a defence against outside incursion or curiosity as the encompassing walls of the home itself. But the social space of the interior contains a number of receding levels of privacy. Its front drawing-room becomes the public within the private, while the emotional terrains of motherhood and family relations are torn between façade and repression. Hidden away as invisible and unspeakable, at the point where the private becomes the secret, is the sphere of sexuality. The repression of the sexual within the private citizen's home is complemented by another hidden world, the underworld of the big city, the marginal area outside the ordered opposition between public and private, between consumption and production, between male and female.

The workplace is no threat to the home. The two maintain each other in a safe, mutually dependent polarisation. The threat comes from elsewhere, from the seething mass of the urban environment, from its working-class tenements and, most of all, from its night-time pleasures. Over and over again, the mysterious, fascinating and frightening image of the city recurs throughout the nineteenth century. It represents an outside to the rule of order. To the individual swallowed up in the crowd, to the law in the refuge given to the criminal, to morality faced with a profusion of bars and prostitutes, the city at night epitomises chaos and uncertainty. The image of the city was that of the jungle, and the detective story came into existence with an adventurer hero who could penetrate and interpret it. Popular entertainment was part of this world but also reflected on it and expressed another side of its contradictions. The misery of the urban masses presented another 'outside' to the private citizen that was easily conflated with criminality and degeneracy, and the sites of entertainment were a manifestation of the chaotic working or unemployed crowd, a liminal world outside order and discipline to be shunned above all by the bourgeois woman and her family.

The early ninteeenth-century melodrama presented a different moral and political perspective. The experience of the city presented dangers, but ones that needed to be represented, interpreted and understood by the poor undergoing the miseries and traumas of early industrial urbanisation.

Innocence (a vanished moral heritage from the village) is tainted and lost in the world of London, a world of moral squalor and physical and mental suffering, as well as the spectacle of life. Hundreds of nineteenth-century plays deal with this theme and scores of them name that City of Dreadful Night in their titles. These plays teem with the life and people of the streets, of the homeless poor, of the cheap lodging houses, the taverns, the gambling dens, and the cold pavement beneath Waterloo Bridge.[10]

The melodrama's narratives caught the irrational reality of

city life and class exploitation with the sharp turns of fortune in plot dependence on coincidence, and a sharp, vivid division between good and evil. But the industrialised city that produced both the Manichaean view of the masses and that of the private citizen began to negotiate a new terrain of the imagination, a popular culture of general melodramatic appeal.

The crowd – no subject was more entitled to the interest of the nineteenth century writers. It was getting ready to take shape as a public in broad strata who had acquired the facility of reading: it wished to find itself portrayed in the contemporary novel . . . Victor Hugo was the first to address the crowd in his titles *Les Miserables, Les Travailleures de la Mer.* In France, Hugo was the only writer able to compete with the serial novel. As is generally known, Eugene Sue was the master of the genre, which began to be a source of revelation to the man in the street. In 1850, an overwhelming majority of working men elected him to Parliament as the representative of the city of Paris.[11]

By the second half of the century, social changes in Britain were indicating a new pattern that would shift the mythology of class relations within the city and male/female relations within the proletariat. The division between home and workplace that had formally characterised the bourgeois private citizen began to extend to other areas of society:

Workers (had) generally lived in the immediate vicinity of their work. Political discussion, drinking and conviviality took place either at the work-place itself or at the local pub which served as a house of all and a centre for union organisation . . . In the second half of the century, this work centered culture began to yield to a culture orientated towards the family and the home. . . By the mid 1870s, weekly hours of work had been substantially reduced in most skilled trades . . . the growth of sea-side excursions, sporting interests, working men's clubs and music-halls from about this time is not accidental. In London, however, this increase in leisure time should be seen in connection with another tendency – the growing separation between home and work-place. . . Increased earnings were not generally spent in late drinking customs but handed over to the wife who became the decision maker in all aspects of household expenditure.[12]

The irreconcilable opposition between the respectable privacy of the bourgeois home and the 'other' world of the urban poor gradually eroded and, in the sphere of mass entertainment, the new entrepreneurs ensured respectability; a safe passage out of the home towards a stable class position within a national consensus culture.

Aesthetics

'A jump from the Hollywood melodrama of the 1950s to the early nineteenth-century theatrical melodrama brackets a particular strand of popular culture, from its birth in the crowded city streets to its death in the television dominated home'. A comparison between the two, very different, melodramatic modes should raise questions about language and expression. Problems of articulation are crucial in a popular culture where the struggle to speak from and about the margins is constantly displaced under the centifugal forces of commercial expansion and censorship. Peter Brooks's chapters on the nineteenth-century melodrama in *The Melodramatic Imagination* make an illuminating juxtaposition with Thomas Elsaesser's invaluable article on Hollywood melodrama *Tales of Sound and Fury*. Both argue that a melodramatic style of aesthetic value and significance exists in its own right. Both associate the formal characteristics of the style with a crisis of expression, in which language is either inappropriate or inadequate to the emotional burden of the subject matter at stake. Both point out the links between the melodramatic mode of expression and the language of the unconscious which must speak through symptom, on the knife-edge between meaning and silence, demanding interpretation rather than a direct, unmediated understanding of what is said.

When the melodramatic form emerged in Paris in the aftermath of the Revolution, it was quickly imported and had an immediate impact on the London working class. The popular theatre of the early nineteenth century was a product of Britain's division into two nations, in which the ruling class extended its hegemony to a divided culture. Under the Licensing Act only three theatres in London were allowed to perform 'legitimate' drama, described later by the actor/manager William McCready as 'plays of poetic quality and supposed literary worth'. The popular ' illegitimate' theatre was defined in precise opposition to the qualities that characterised high cultural production. The law ensured that it should be non-literary entertainment in which words must be accompanied by music. Command over language, reading, writing and authoritative speech is a mark of political and economic dominance. But out of these circumstances the melodrama developed an important aesthetic of its own that bears witness to the energy of contemporary popular culture. The plays were watched by massive audiences of London's poor in theatres that could hold two thousand or more. Dickens describes the magical transition from chaos and tumult to hushed attention as the play started.

Peter Brooks's argument shows how the melodrama's aesthetic strength lies precisely in its displacement of the power of the word. This ' low cultural' form can reflect on human struggle with language and expression, and thus have an important influence on the development of Romantic theatre. The aesthetics of the popular melodrama depend on grand gesture, tableaux, broad moral themes, with narratives of coincidence, reverses and sudden happy endings organised around rigid opposition between good and evil. Characters represent forces rather than people, and fail to control or understand their circumstances so that fate, rather than heroic transcendence, offers a resolution to the drama. A highly inflected narrative of passion and surprise must replace word with gesture and language with a visual representation of meaning. While the aesthetics of melodrama evolved for a non-literate audience, the style both throws doubt on the adequacy of speech to express the complexities of passion and, instead, offers a wide range of semantic alternatives: 'Gestures in all forms is a necessary complement and supplement to the word, tableau is a repeated device in the summary of meaning acted out, and the mute role of the virtuoso is an emblem of the possibilities of meaning engendered in the absence of the word.'[13] A whole terrain of the 'unspeakable' can thus be depicted.

The melodramatic style had a strong influence on the cinema, partly through the genealogy that links different moments in the development of popular theatrical spectacle. But also, the movies were born mute, distanced from language by technology rather than the law. These constraints placed a similar emphasis on gesture, dramatic action, and expression through visual meaning. Even the tableau's elongation of time is reflected in the cinematic convention of intercutting between looks and gestures within a scene, so extending the possibilities for audience reading and interpretation. This cinematic style survived, along with musical accompaniment, expression through colour and lighting and *mise-en-scène* so that the popular cinema is suffused with the traditions of melodrama far beyond the particular genre that has inherited its name.

The Hollywood melodrama throws new light on an aesthetic which had its origins in the previous century. On the cinematic level, the Hollywood melodrama's use of stylised performance, *mise-en-scène* and so on is aesthetically more reminiscent of the silent cinema than its own contemporaries. But the subject matter that defines the genre, associated above all with woman, the family, the home, passion etc., suggests a further relation to the melodramatic style and the 'texts of Muteness'. Peter Brooks argues that the early melodrama's language of signs relates it to the language of the unconscious. The drama foregrounds material that evades conscious articulation: 'mute gesture is an expressionistic means – precisely the means of melodrama – to render meanings that are ineffable, but none the less operative in the sphere of human ethical relationships'.[14] In the 1950s family drama this relationship becomes more explicit. Its setting, the family, touches directly on the raw nerve of the psychoanalytic. The social sphere of the family provides a ready-made *dramatis personae* of characters whose relations are by very definition overdetermined and overlaid with tension and contradiction, destined to act out Oedipal drama, generational conflict, sibling rivalry, the containment and repression of sexuality. At one and the same time, the family is the socially accepted road to respectable normality, an icon of conformity, and the source of deviance, psychosis and despair. In addition to these elements of dramatic raw material, the family provides a physical setting, the home, that can hold a drama in claustrophobic intensity and represent, with its highly connotative architectural organisation, the passions and antagonisms that lie behind it. Here the text of muteness is produced not by the material constraints of the law or technology but by a proximity to the mechanisms of repression, that is aggravated in, for instance, the suburban expansion of Eisenhower's America with its desperate concern for appearances.

Thomas Elsaesser giver a further aesthetic dimension to the Hollywood melodramatic style. He distinguishes the cinema of cathartic action from the cinema of the domestic interior, which acts as a space that confines rather than providing a wide terrain for escape and realised conflict. The space of the home can then relate metaphorically, to the inside space of human interiority, emotions and the unconscious.

In one case, the drama moves forward to its resulution by having the central conflicts successively externalised and projected into direct action. A jail-break, a bank robbery, a Western chase or cavalry charge and even a criminal investigation all lend themselves to psychologised, thematised representations of the heroes' inner dilemmas . . . Not so in the domestic melodrama: the social pressures are such, the frame of respectability so sharply defined that the range of 'strong' actions is limited. The tellingly impotent gesture, the social gaffe, the hysterical outburst replaces any more directly liberating or self-annihilating action and the cathartic violence of a shoot-out or chase becomes an inner violence, often one which the characters turn against themselves. The dramatic configuration, the pattern of the plot makes them, regardless of any attempt to break free, constantly look inwards, at each other and themselves.[15]

This sense of overdetermined gesture is there when Kyle Hadley throws his whisky at his mirror image, when Cary Scott breaks the Wedgwood pot that Ron has so painstakingly mended for her, when Sara-Jane Johnson kicks Susie's little white lamb across the floor. But in addition to the actions of individual characters, the constraints of plot, setting and expression spill over on to the cinematic image itself, so that meaning is infused into objects, colours, lighting, framing, camera movement, and so on.

Hollywood has considerably naturalised the mode of performance associated with the theatrical melodrama. The family melodrama, however, produces a new variant of self-conscious, stylised acting. Through social and generic logic, the melodrama produces a preponderance of female protagonists. The presence of this woman, in contradiction with her sexuality, suffering from passion and repression, is in an uneasy tension with the conventions that order woman's image on the screen as erotic object of visual pleasure. As sexuality is presented as a problem, its easy veneer falls away in pieces. The protagonist, with whom our sympathy and understanding lie, is subjected to the curious and prurient gaze of intrusive community, neighbours, friends and family so that the spectator's own look becomes self-conscious and awkward. A conventional expectation of pleasure is transformed into embarrassment. Fassbinder uses this distanciation device in *Fear Eats the Soul*, his remake of Douglas Sirk's *All That Heaven Allows*. (He also elongates the last moments of particular scenes into tableaux reminiscent of the nineteenth-century theatrical melodrama.) In the Holly-wood melodrama there is a delicate balance between the protagonists' self-consciousness and the actresses' mastery over a self-conscious performance. This is achieved above all, perhaps, by Lana Turner acting Lora Meredith acting being an actress in *Imitation of Life*.

Feminist theory of popular culture has concentrated on the processes that produce the image of woman as 'signifier of sexuality' and has striven to create a sexual politics around representation that displaces and alters previous discourses. Significantly, feminism has also concentrated political atten-tion on women's place in the home and family. Throughout, words, written and spoken, have been a political weapon for the Women's Movement, from the days of consciousness-raising to recent feminist preoccupation with linguistic and psychoanalytic theory. The question of how and where women are positioned in relation to language and dominant cultural production has highlighted women's marginality, near silence, and different, dispersed moves towards hesitant speech. This is not to say that women are, or at any point were, outside language (or the law) but that a given, limited vocabulary, characteristic of the oppressed, simply failed to provide the words needed to articulate the experience of oppression . . . A shift towards a collective ability to articu-late is a crucial political step, but what is said and how this speech relates to that of the 'centre' has continued or increased importance. There is a moment that might approxi-mate to the threshold of speech, where conscious articulation is prefigured by the oblique forms of metaphor, symbolism and a complex, semiotically charged, system which implies desire for political, conscious realisation of oppression in language. This chapter has intended to argue that the

moment of threshold in popular spectacular entertainment
has been turned away from speaking for oppressed groups
by the centrifugal forces of national consensus, which then
represent their interests and welfare and improved conditions
of life with accompanying cultural loss. Paradoxically, this
process has been negotiated primarily through an appeal to
the figure of the mother as 'signifier of censorship', which
then comes to complement the eroticised image of woman
that signifies only male desire and cannot speak woman's
desire. There are two strands of silence at stake here, doubling
up and intertwined like a double helix: the mother's
mythologised image as censorship and the mother's own
containment and constraint within the language of patriarchal domination. The complex processes and cultural patterns at stake here might just be breaking apart as the long
standing tradition of tension between inside and outside is
resolved, television finally bringing popular entertainment
into the home.

Television arrived within the home, within censorship, for
a family audience, tailored to front parlour size. It also challenged the previous, well established separation between
public and private by turning political events into spectacular
drama acted out within the confines of the home. Television
was well and truly launched in the US by two events
symptomatic of the conservatism that swept the country in
the early fifties: the televised McCarthy hearings, and the
televised proceedings of the United Nations investigation
into the Korean War. It arrives with the backing and presence
of national authority, without any awkward, difficult period
on the limits that must have marked its predecessors. It represents the triumph of the home as point of consumption
of capitalist circulation of commodities. But, at the same
time, the apparent resolution of contradiction may well indicate a change in history, and the forces that coalesce
economics with culture and sexual/psychoanalytic structures.
During the 1950s the mother was challenged as the only

source of commodity spending power by her teenage children. At the same time, the youth market and its ancillary sectors turned towards their own cultural spheres, leading gradually to a new break-up of the old centrifugal forces of consensus centralisation. In the music market, for instance, small companies can, for some time at least, resist the pull of the major producers and distributors; 16 mm film has made film-making available to women's groups and political activists; video gives people control over what they see on their television screens. At the same time the national consensus is itself being threatened from above, literally from the sky, by satellite broadcasting that challenges legal and national boundaries. It seems appropriate that both threats to national broadcasting should be seen in terms of, or constitute, a sexual threat to the integrity of the home. Both video boom and satellite have been associated with an influx of pornography. Once again this rhetoric conceals the real contradictions, the dangers and possibilities that are hidden in these historical developments.

Notes

1 Judith Mayne, 'Immigrants and spectators', *Wide Angle* 5, 2.

2 John Halliday, *Sirk on Sirk* (London: Secker and Warburg, 1971).

3 Rem Koolhaas, *Delirious New York* (London: Acamemy Editions, 1978) p. 38.

4 Albert F. McLean, *American Vaudeville as Ritual* (Lexington: Univesity of Kentucky Press, 1965), p. 31.

5 *Ibid.,* p. 93.

6 Koolhaas, *op. cit.,* p. 35.

7 McLean, *op. cit,* p. 31.

8 Russell Merritt, 'Nickelodeon theatres 1905-1914: building an audience for the movies', in *The American Film Industry,* Tino Balio ed. (Madison: University of Wisconsin Press, 1976), pp. 72-3.

9 Walter Benjamin: *Charles Baudelaire* (London: New Left Books, 1973), p. 167.

10 Michael Booth ed. *The Magistrate and Other Nineteenth Century Plays.* (London: Oxford University Press, 1974), p. ix.

11 Walter Benjamin, *op. cit.,* p. 120.

12 Gareth Steadman Jones, *Languages of Class,* (Cambridge: Cambridge University Press, 1983) pp. 217-18.

13 Peter Brooks, *The Melodramatic Imagination,* (New York: Columbia

University Press, 1985), p. 62.
14 *Ibid.*, p. 73.
15 Thomas Elsaesser, 'Tales of sound and fury', *Monogram* 1, 4, p. 9.

Narrative form in American network television

Theories of television narrative have attempted to situate the television 'apparatus' both in its continuity with earlier narrative forms and in its difference from them. Much British television theory appears to accept the premise that

like cinema, television is an apparatus used for the production-reproduction of the novelistic; it serves to address the problem of the definition of forms of individual meaning within the limits of existing social representations and their determining social relations, the provision and maintenance of terms of social intelligibility for the individual.[1]

Certainly, in a broad historical sense, one cannot take exception to this claim. However, to follow out this line of reasoning is to stress television's similarity to the novel and cinema, rather than its differences from other narrative forms. In what follows, I will stress theories of difference over those of continuity, since I believe that television[2] as an apparatus differs in almost every significant respect from cinema. Television is not very well described by models of narrative analysis based on linearity and resolution. Nor is its metapsychology that of the cinema. According to Rick Altman,

Whereas the level of audience attention to a given Hollywood film scene may be roughly dependent on the importance of that scene for resolving the plot's dilemmas, attention to a given *Dallas* scene depends instead on the topic and characters present. In recognition of this difference, we might say that classical Hollywood narrative is in large part *goal-driven*, while attention to American television narrative is heavily *menu-driven*.[3]

If the historical subject for the novel and cinema has been the isolated individual 'reader/spectator', then the subject interpellated by television has been always already familial.

Television narrative structure

Most theories of cinematic narrative have stressed a linear, causal model derived from the work of Roland Barthes and others. That this is the dominant model for conceptualising cinematic narrative is illustrated by a definition of 'narrative' given in a popular film introductory text as 'a chain of events in cause/effect relationship occuring in time.'[4] Following Barthes, the narrative structure of the classical Hollywood text is seen as proceeding through a chain of narrative 'enigmas' towards closure. Although much criticism has been levelled at such a totalising theory of cinematic narrative (not the least because it describes masculine genres better than feminine genres) I believe that it is even less applicable to the operation of television. The television apparatus works against logical notions of causality and closure. According to John Ellis, television narrative operates through the segment, i.e. a relatively self-contained scene that is discontinuous with other segments. Ellis goes on to argue that 'movement from one segment to the next is a matter of succession rather than consequence'. Thus, for Ellis, all television narrative is *serial* rather than linear, in the sense that 'the series implies the form of the dilemma rather than that of resolution and closure'.[5] In this sense, neither of the two forms of television narrative that I will discuss – the episodic series and the continuing serial – correspond to the dominant model of popular cinematic narrative. However, their methods of non-correspondence differ.

Metapsychology

The dominant model of the 'cinematic apparatus' based on the work of Metz, Baudry and others does not account very well for television. Television may be seen to possess a different 'imaginary' from cinema, to articulate a different position for its subject, and to demand ways of looking which do not correspond to mirror-identification and voyeurism as they have been described for the cinema. In another context, I have argued that so-called magazine format nonfiction television sets up an idealised quasi-nuclear family whose unity is seen as an attribute of the medium itself.[6] This representational strategy has its completion in the mode of address of the apparatus – 'from our family to yours'. (These are the actual words used in the Christmas message sent to 'my family' by the local news 'team' in my market.) That is to say that the 'implied spectator' for television is not the isolated, immobilised pre-Oedipal individual described by Metz and Baudry in their metapsychology of the cinema, but rather a post-Oedipal, fully socialised family member. Thus we need to revise a model of specularity derived from the cinema by providing for television a new destination to Metz's quest in *The Imaginary Signifier* for an analogue to the Lacanian mirror.[7] For television, we would have to dispute or at least reformulate Metz's claim that the spectator's own body is never reflected in the mirror. To be perversely literal-minded (in keeping with the spirit of much metapsychological speculation of this ilk), the television screen *does* reflect the body of the family, if we turn the images off. This is perhaps a metaphorical way of arguing that the representational content of television proposes a reflection, however distorted, of the body of the familialised viewing subject. We are not dealing with the same degree of signification-by-absence that can be deduced from an examination of the 'basic cinematographic apparatus' if only because, as I have argued at length elsewhere, television disseminates an ideology of presence that has its basis in the presumed 'live' status of the apparatus.[8]

By extension, the unevenly developed dialectic of voyeurism and exhibitionism that Metz theorises for the cinema
does not operate with the same force for television. Far from
wanting to disguise its discourse as story, television seems
to want to foreground its discursive status. As Robert Stam
has written regarding television news, 'if illusionistic fictions
disguise their discourse as history, television news, in certain
respects, wraps up its history as discourse'.[9] This calls into
question a model of spectatorship based upon voyeurism.
Television's foremost illusion is that it is an *interactive
medium*, not that we are peering into a self-enclosed diegetic
space. This generalised stance of the apparatus as a whole,
due in part to the property of 'flow', tends to carry over to
the more cinematic narrative modes of the episodic series
and the continuing serial, if only because these 'diegetic'
fictions are continually interrupted (especially on American
television) by more discursive structures in the form of voice-
over announcements, commercials, and promotional 'spots'.
The 'diegesis' in television can never be sustained in the
imaginary of the cinema either at a narrative level or at the
level of modes of reception. As Raymond Williams has
explained, the historically determined mode of reception for
television in the West depends upon a social use of technology 'which served an at once mobile and home-centred way
of living: a form of *mobile privatisation*'.[10] This is in sharp
contrast to the psychoanalytical view of the historical conditions
of reception for theatrical cinema which might be described as
'immobilised public consumption'. In this regard, it is important
to take into account studies which demonstrate the viewer's 'talking back' to television – a process now literalised on certain cable
systems by interactive cable capability, but also an implied feature
of network television. The very concept 'diegesis' is unthinkable
on television. One rather astonishing example of television's
tendency to 'break' the cinematic diegesis (that I have observed
recently) is a pattern of interrupting the ten o'clock drama with

'promos' for the eleven o'clock local news in which the news anchors, in direct address, attempt to draw parallels between the presumed diegetic fiction and a 'real' happening that will be 'covered' in the forthcoming news broadcast. For example, a 'news report' on college students' ritualistic viewing of *Dynasty* was announced during the commercial break preceding the last segment of *Dynasty* and then broadcast during the news report directly following *Dynasty*. Similarly, following a 'trauma drama' on teen suicide, the eleven o'clock news announced and subsequently presented 'expert' psychological advice on how to recognise suicidal tendencies in 'your' children. The example appears all the more bizarre if considered in terms of screen theory, when one recognises that the identical 'expert advice' had already been given within the diegesis of the made-for-TV film in the form of a public address to a self-help group given by the mother of one of the dead children. Yet it does not appear bizarre to the viewing subject thus addressed precisely because such disregard for the diegetic is a *conventional* television practice, not an exceptional one. Television as an ideological apparatus strives to break down any barriers between the fictional diegesis, the advertising diegesis, and the diegesis of the viewing family, finding it advantageous to assume all three are one and the same.

Familialised Technology

In order to deal with differences within American network television's representational mode, a good place to begin would be in the different strategies for dealing with 'the family', both at the level of narration and that of mode of reception. Although both the episodic series and the continuing serial are serial forms constituted by the media's economically derived need for perpetual self-reduplication, they differ in their narrative strategies. The self-replication of the episodic series depends upon a continual re-integration of the family; that of the continuing serial depends upon a continual disintegration of the family.

In almost Lévi-Straussian terms, the dominant binary opposition informing television's representational practices is that of inside the family/outside the family. Both the episodic series and the continuing serial have as their 'irresolvable' cultural contradiction the need to explain factors which in reality are 'outside' in terms of the 'inside'. For television, both the economic and the socio-political cannot be thought except in terms of 'inside the family' – an impossible dilemma, if indeed such dilemmas cannot be resolved inside the family. The social may not be equivalent to the familiar, but for ideological reasons, television's narrative representations would have it so. Here we must part company with Lévi-Strauss, in order to note that the inability to resolve the inside/outside contradiction is not a universal attribute of the human mind but rather an ideological construct derived from the social formation as a whole and buttressed by the specific role of the television apparatus as a mechanism for reproducing ideology. Thus the television 'apparatus' is historically determined.

Recent revisionist broadcast historians have emphasised the extent to which a *social* conception of broadcast technology influenced the development of that technology in the direction of Williams's 'mobile privatisation'. According to these historians, the technology by no means determined its innovation as an apparatus for private consumption within the family. In its experimental period, television's initial location was in the public theatre, and it was primarily its association with radio that led to television's innovation as a home-based advertising media in America.[11] Radio itself had been instrumental in the growth of consumerism, the process of changing the American home into a unit for consumption rather than production. In this changing ideology of the home, the radio receiver played a significant role in conferring status.[12] Whereas the radio industry had initially sought in the family a market for its receiving equipment (as had the BBC in its formative years), the American radio manufacturers from their first attempts to innovate television in the 1930s already had in mind a model for selling families to advertisers. This socio-economic relationship between the apparatus and the familial viewing subject has its counterpart in television's textual strategies.

The episodic series

As an example of the mode of representation of the episodic series, I will discuss its simplest and least cinematic genre – the situation comedy. In the early 1970s two conceptions of the sitcom family competed for dominance on American network TV. The Norman Lear sitcoms (*All in the Family, Maude, The Jeffersons*) dealt with nuclear families beset from the outside by a variety of socially-derived problems. This ideological conflict which each week would spring from a new source or 'enigma' would split the family apart, usually dividing neatly along progressive v. reactionary lines. Typically, *All in the Family* would provide two axes along which 'secondary identifications' could be made – the reactionary father v. the liberal children – thus making the Lear sitcom epitomise a 'liberal' narrative strategy, based on balance and a 'choice' of objects for identification. By the end of each episode, the specific 'enigma of the week' would be resolved, with the underlying social problem (usually involving racial or feminist issues) retained as an 'absent cause' for the ensuing series episode. The Lear family, however much they were divided along political lines, would each week be reintegrated in order that a new enigma could be introduced. The Lear sitcom thus politicised the basic sitcom structure of a return to equilibrium and a new dilemma which would proceed in an endless circle until the series was cancelled.

The alternate 1970s paradigm, the family of co-workers, was a product of MTM Enterprises' sitcom factory. Here the dilemmas tended to be interpersonal or 'lifestyle' issues which made a better transition than the Lear programmes into the apolitical late *1970*s (e.g. *Taxi, Cheers*). If the Lear sitcom implied that solutions within the family were but a means of temporary weekly closure, the MTM sitcom stressed the unity of the family above all other values. The substitution of the work family for the nuclear family actually aided in this task, since its all-encompassing nature provided no avenues of escape. It also provided a 'mirror' family that was at once more realistic and more Utopian – realistic in that the nuclear family was no longer the dominant form outside the texts; Utopian in that love and work merged in an essentially harmonious universe that represented a throwback to a less corporate age – a residual ideology. A typical situation on *The Mary Tyler Moore Show* would involve a threat to the unity of the family that would be resolved when the recalcitrant family member realised that family unity represents a higher goal than personal ambition. For example, for each of the main characters, an episode featured the dilemma of taking a new job that would mean withdrawal from the work-family; in each case the character is unable at the last moment to 'leave home' and the episode ends in a group celebration of the reintegration of the family. When a major character actually did depart, she would be replaced by a new family member, thus keeping the work/family balance stable.

The dominant view of the episodic series sitcom as essentially static and conservative is argued in David Grote's *The End of Comedy*.[13] Following Northrop Frye's conception of the comic mode, Grote's argument is based on a distinction between the comic mode of the television sitcom and Grote's idiosyncratic view of the 2,000 years of dramatic comedy preceeding it. According to Grote, the enduring form of 'new comedy' was anarchic in that it continually retold the story of a regeneration of the social order through the rebellion of a young couple against the authority of the father. The sitcom, by contrast, resists not only the change of the traditional comic plot but *all* change of any kind. According to Grote, the sitcom carries its repetition compulsion to such an extreme that it has all but rejected the concept of plot as a process of change from an old equilibrium to a new. His description of the process by which narrative development is avoided supports the view that television series narrative is essentially circular. The sitcom, he says, never reaches a new equilibrium but only returns to that point of stasis from which the episode began. From this static narrative economy, Grote deduces that the moral lesson of the sitcom is that all problems can be solved within the family. Changes of mind and solutions to problems all happen to outsiders who must be expelled by the end of each episode. Thus the reintegration of the sitcom family is bought at the cost of narrative and ideological stasis.

Grote's view of the sitcom's handling of the inside/outside the family contradiction might be that one side of the binary opposition (the outside) is, through the narrative mechanism of the sitcom plot, erased. We are left with a pure interiority and a monolithically conservative view of social relations. We can then contrast this to the developmental mode of the continuing serial in which both situations and characters change and grow organically, thus setting up another neat binary opposition between a reactionary form (the sitcom) and a progressive form (the continuing serial). That this is an attractive interpretation is proven by the popularity of this view in both journalistic and academic circles.

However, much is omitted in this easy explanation, most significantly any theory of how the sitcom is *read* by its audience. Grote is unable to explain how an audience that for 2,000 years was able to accept a progressive form of comedy could – in about twenty years – get 'hooked' on such a static, anti-progressive form and then, in the space of about five years, become subjects for an entirely new developmental form of narrative art – the continuing serial drama. Such a rapid public acceptance of an overarching diachronic transformation of the narrative apparatus of American network television is the historical 'fact' that an undialectical view such as Grote's is unable to explain. Instead of viewing changes in narrative forms as breaks in essentially synchronic structures, I believe we must view the transformation from the episodic series to the continuing serial both dialectically and historically.

In order to do this, we have to question a monolithically static view of the episodic series at the same time that we qualify the developmental interpretation of serial form. For if the episodic series sitcom was static at the level of situation, it was not so at the level of character (throughout the 1970s). Narrative analysis, however, has taught us to look for change in a rather Proppian fashion as the syntagmatic changes in narrative functions. This kind of change will not be found in the 'pure' episodic series. For example, after seven years, Mary Richards was still encountering the same situations she had in the first season. But Mary had changed in terms of the traits attached to her character, that is, paradigmatically. If we examine the credit sequences for the first, second, and ensuing seasons, this change is apparent in that the initial enigma shifts from the future conditional to the future indicative tense (you might just make it after all/ you're gonna make it after all). After this, the question 'how will you make it on your own?' is dropped altogether; presumably it is no longer in question.

Another factor that the concentration on plot functions overlooks is that the static nature of the family-integration plot is not without its progressive aspects. The fact that Mary's situation could not develop very much should not be seen in an entirely negative light. For it meant that Mary could never leave the Utopian work/family in order to settle down into bourgeois domesticity. After the pilot episode, there was never any question of Mary attaching herself to a particular man. In many respects, the family of co-workers represented a progressive alternative – in its integration of the public and domestic spheres, in its emphasis on reciprocity within independence, and its valuing of the collective experience of the ensemble. For the spectator, especially the 'new woman' audience for which this programme had a special meaning, the family in the mirror was a Utopian one that deserved to remain together. Here we must question Grote's tendency to read Frye in the most strongly developmental way possible. Although Frye says that 'the theme of the comic is the integration of society, which usually takes the form of incorporating a central character into it', he does not say that movement toward a *more* Utopian society is inevitable in comedy.[14] And there is a sense in which the reintegration of the family each week *does* represent 'development'.

The continuing serial

Given the sitcom's potential for diachronic development in the direction of character growth and change, we should view the greater diachronic development of the American sitcom in the 1980s as part of the general movement on American television towards the continuing serial form, not as an abrupt break with the static series format. A number of developments within television programming during the mid-1970s provided the transition to the continuing serial. First, as I have already mentioned, sitcoms began to move toward a more developmental model, so that by the early 1980s it was possible for a sitcom such as *Cheers* to modify even the basic situation (i.e. Diane's and Sam's enmity). Secondly, in two crucial programmes – *Mary Hartman* and *Soap*, comedy and melodrama were combined in a continuing serial format. Thirdly, continuing daytime serials became very popular; and peak-time melodramas emerged with *Dallas*. At the same time, certain peak-time melodramatic series types (the 'cop show' and the medical drama) began to take on the continuing serial format. Thus we have to explain and correlate a double transformation – from the comic to the melodramatic and form the series to the serial.

Mary Hartman and *Soap* both illustrate that when the sitcom moved in the direction of the continuing serial, it also took on a more melodramatic flavour. One possible explanation for this is that comedy tends to stress integration and closure, whereas melodrama has always stressed disintegration and an 'unsatisfying' or ambiguous sense of closure. But the self-replication of the continuing serial cannot depend upon integration. In order to keep the various plot lines going, disintegration must be the method of self-replication. In the continuing serial, as exemplified by the daytime soap opera, the inside/outside the family contradiction has always been expressed in terms of the disintegration of the family. This is not to imply that circumstances outside the familial have any greater force. As Tania Modleski has stated, the main fantasy of the soap opera remains that of a fully self-sufficient family.[15] The difference is that whereas in the MTM sitcom that family is constantly regenerated in a Utopian fashion, in the continuing melodramatic serial the integrated family is a goal whose achievement would mean the end of the hermeneutic chain. We cannot say that the movement toward the continuing serial *caused* a change towards melodrama, or vice versa. Rather, it seems logical that the two should have been articulated together.[16] Since I have discussed the dynamics of the continuing serial elsewhere,[17] I would like to proceed directly to the implications of the transition to the continuing serial as form-in-dominance. For different reasons a number of analysts have wanted to describe this change as 'progressive'. However, all (including myself) have tended to confuse a *narrative* sense of 'progress' with a political sense of the term. For the industry and the popular press that perpetuates its views, serials are progressive in that they affirm bourgeois notions of character development and growth. We can reject this explanation at two levels – first, it is arguable that a static conception of character is a more damning description of bourgeois social relations. Secondly, it is not correct to say that characters *change* in continuing serials. Quite the contrary – they perpetuate the narrative by continuing to make the same mistakes. Rather, due to the multiple plot structure, characters' *positions* shift in relation to other characters. To quote Rick Altman, '*Dallas* is organised not according to a novelistic hermeneutic, but around an intricate menu of topics which for some viewers are experienced by character and for others by theme'.[18] The diachronic development of continuing serials depends more upon the shifting status of the various couples and families. At any given synchronic moment, families that were once integrated are now disintegrated, and vice-versa. Integration into a happy family remains the ultimate goal, but it cannot endure for any given couple. The various sets of couples achieve in fulcrum fashion a balance between harmony and disharmony, but no one couple can remain in a state of integration (or of disintegration).

My discussion of the sitcom makes clear that 'misreadings' are eminently possible; indeed the 'liberal' structure of the Lear sitcom ensured differential readings of Archie's racism. However, I would still maintain that the emphasis upon reintegration of the family does not allow much space for a critique of the nuclear family structure itself. (However, one might read the substitution of the Utopian work family as constituting a form of critique.)

For the continuing serial, the very need to 'rupture' the family in order for the plot to continue can be viewed as a 'dangerous' strategy in the sense that it allows for a reading of the disintegration as a critique of the family itself. Specifically, it threatens to explode the strategy of containment common to both the series and serial by which all conflicts are expressed in terms of the family. In the sitcom, the threatening forces are re-expelled each week. The continuing serial, by contrast, maintains its 'outside' within the family structure. The outside forces which threaten the sitcom family become the inside forces which threaten the internal disintegration of the continuing serial family. In allowing the family to be perennially torn apart, there is always the danger that 'the outside' will explode upon the inside. We cannot, however, guarantee that this will lead to *politically* progressive readings of continuing serials. Rather than set up an opposition between the episodic series and the continuing serial along reactionary/radical lines, I would prefer to view them as two different responses to television's dual ideological compulsions: the need to repeat and the need to contain.

Notes

1 Stephen Heath and Gillian Skirrow, 'Television: a world in action', *Screen* 18, summer 1977.

2 I refer to American commercial television and to some British programming.

3 'Television/Sound', paper delivered at the Society for Cinema Studies Conference, Madison, Wisconsin, March 1984.

4 David Bordwell and Kristin Thompson, *Film Art: An Introduction* (Reading, Mass: Addison-Wesley, 1979).

5 John Ellis, *Visible Fictions* (London: Routledge and Kegan Paul, 1982), pp. 145-60.

6 'The concept of live TV: ontology as ideology', in E. Ann Kaplan, ed., *Regarding Television* (Fredrick, Maryland: University Publications of America, 1983), pp. 12-22.

7 Christian Metz, *The Imaginary Signifier* (Bloomington: Indiana University Press, 1975), pp. 1-88.

8 Kaplan, *op. cit.*

9 'Television news and its spectator', in Kaplan, ed., *op. cit.*, p. 38.

10 *Television: Technology and Cultural Form* (New York: Schocken Books, 1975), p. 26.

11 Jeanne Allen, 'The social matrix of television: invention in the U.S.', In Kaplan, *op. cit.*

12 Willian Boddy, 'The rhetoric and the economic roots of the American broadcast industry', *Cine-Tracts* 2, spring, 1979.

13 Hamden, Connecticut: The Shoestring Press, 1983.

14 *Anatomy of Criticism* (Princeton, New Jersey: Princeton University Press, 1957), p. 43.

15 *Loving with a Vengeance*, (New York and London: Methuen, 1984).

16 We also need to conceptualise the historical and cultural factors influencing the shift in narrative paradigms beyond the obvious observation that the 'mood' of the country had 'swung' from liberal to conservative.

17 'Melodrama, serial form and television today', *Screen* 25 Jan./Feb. 1984, pp. 4-18.

18 See note 3.

Hellivision:
an analysis of video games

Dissection

In investigating popular culture the only way not to feel like a snooping health visitor, sniffing out whether someone's environment is fit to live in, is to examine some aspect or form of it which evokes passionate feelings in oneself. For me video games are both fetish and phobia, since at one level I am fascinated by the control involved in being able to relate to and interact with a text on the video screen, but at the level of the content of the games I am repelled. So in this chapter I want to dissect the games to take out their pleasures and, after the disembowelment, to try to read what the entrails predict for the future relationship between gender and uses of the new technology in both its popular entertainment and its business forms. For the pleasure of video games is gender-specific – women do not play them – and it seems important when studying popular culture to examine not only what pleasures arise at different historical periods, but for whom. The materiality of the relationship between text and spectator is nowhere clearer than in video games, where the spectator is also the performer, and performance involves learning a skill which will give the player an advantage over the non-player in the market for creative computer jobs as opposed to clerical, key-punching work. So in looking at the video games the study of effects and the study of pleasure will be the same thing.

History

The structure of video games nearly always conforms to a truncated version of the folk-tale form analysed by Propp: a lack provides the motivation for a hero to struggle with a villain which leads either to defeat for the hero (unusual in folk-tales but very common in video games) or to his victory and return. In computer circles, however, it is widely believed that the origin of video games lies in the war games which have been a popular form of entertainment since the seventeenth century. In war games the emphasis is not on an individual hero but on the environment in which a battle is to be fought. During the 1960s books of rules were published to use with war games which described a detailed environment to the players, usually set in one of four main periods: ancient, medieval, Napoleonic, or modern. Some games were still played with model armies, but board games were also developed, and – perhaps in tune with a general move towards the dramatisation of life – there evolved the role-playing game. One of the most successful of these games was *Dungeons and Dragons,* published by Tactical Studies Rules, which was a medieval fantasy. The environment was designed and presided over by a 'dungeon master' (Greimas's 'Destinateur'?) and each player could control one of the several characters: a fighting man, an elf, a wizard, etc. The fascination with a mythical, magical past, as evidenced by the popularity of J. R. R. Tolkien's *Fellowship of the Ring* published in 1954, and a general revival of interest in the occult, can partly be explained as a rebellion against modernity, but partly too it can perhaps be seen as an interest in representations of the almost-forgotten infancy – the magical past – of the individual. Even though the fantasy environments of role-playing games soon included spaces of the future, such as a post-nuclear metropolis or a spaceship, the way of functioning in these spaces was primarily magical – by answering conundrums, for example. Later these games were adapted for a single player, by being put into books as stories with a series of multiple choice questions and with the text as dungeon master. The major work in this form was *Tunnels and Trolls,* a version of which was devised for a mainframe computer.

The commercial development of the games for computer produced a splitting of the games into different categories. First on the scene were arcade games, the most memorable of which is *Space Invaders,* which focused on a real-time engagement with sheets of aliens. The skills called for in the arcade game are mainly fast reaction and good hand-eye co-ordination; the games' other attractions are their brilliant graphics, the laser precision of their weapons, and the very challenging targets which sometimes have unusual propen-sities, such as multiplying by splitting when hit. These games began to be installed in amusement arcades in 1975 and soon had the teenage generation addicted.

Meanwhile, listings for games which called for intelligence rather than physical skill were being published in computer magazines. These eventually found a commercial outlet as management or strategy games. Here the emphasis was on functioning in a technological environment and the games' intentions were apparently playfully didactic. For example, in such a game you might play the part of a ruler of a Third World country who – given so many acres of fertile land, so much grain in store, and so many people – has to balance the ponderables to last as many years as possible before being overtake by famine or revolution.

The adventure game – with which we shall be mostly con-cerned in this essay – has evolved out of a mixture of all these categories, but its particular form has also been partly deter-mined by its distribution system. The arcade game came into the home via games consoles, and their popularity led to games being developed for the home computer, which in turn led to an enormous expansion of the home computer industry. Ninety-five per cent of the software for home computers is now in the form of video games. But the games had to change, partly because the technology of the home computer was not adequate to the precision needed for a satisfactory arcade game, and partly because the owners of home computers were younger than the arcade frequenters and enjoyed a story framework for the battles.

So it was that the war game/folk-tale/comic strip combination became the dominant form through which children learnt computer literacy both at home and in computer clubs at school. But this history has not explained why this particular form of entertainment has captured the popular imagination to the extent of inspiring a feature film – *Tron* – and affecting the form of television commercials, popular music 'promos', and motifs and style in design in general, which however short-lived it proves to be, had a very important effect at the time of the introduction of the new technology. Part of any account of the popularity of video games must be the fact that the games represent very powerfully the breakdown of boundaries characteristic of postmodern culture: boundaries between fantasy and science, between high-tech and primitivism, and between play and real life. But the boundary that I think best explains the games' attraction at this time, and particularly for boys and men, is that between anxiety and pleasure.

Industry

There is a lack of clarity about terminology in the production of video games which reflects an uncertainty about what kind of industry the games are. Sometimes the producing companies are called manufacturers, sometimes publishers, and sometimes producers, but the term that seems to be gaining the widest acceptance is 'software houses', with its overtones of domestic production.

The authorship of the games is similarly indeterminate.

Often, boys write to a software house with a basic idea for which they are paid a fee. They are able to see themselves as authors or writers, certainly as creators, and earners too. There are also specialist writers of games, but the emphasis is often on the team of craftspeople, as in the film industry, who produced the game in its final form with graphics, music, and sound effects. To emphasise the 'glamour' angle, and at the same time apparently to undercut it with parody, the industry has set up its own festival, at Blackpool rather than Cannes, where the Golden Joystick awards are presented. The craft that is most suppressed in the publicity is the key one of the computer programmer.

In the texts of the games themselves uncertainty of origin is made into a virtue. The basic story is often realised through a pastiche of borrowings from other forms of popular culture. Inter-textuality is incorporated into the surprise mechanisms. For example, in the middle of one adventure game a monster called the Gambling Gorilla forces you into a game of *Play Your Cards Right,* an idea borrowed from a television quiz show. News and current affairs, in their media images, also form the subject of some games: *Harrier Attack* was very popular after the Falklands war, and games about political figures such as *Denis Through the Drinking Glass* and *The Tebbit* have had their moments. Euston Films televison series *Minder* has been made into a game, and films such as *Jaws, Death Race* and *Firefox* are reduced to their chase and battle sequences and marketed under the same title. Characters such as Spiderman from boys' comics also have their own adventure games. Other sources include books – especially Tolkien and science fiction, the confession and the diary; fruit machines – there is a game called *Jackpot;* sport – *Horace goes Skiing,* and many motor-bike games, car games, and adaptations of board games; toys – as in Bear Bovver (a horror version of the teddy bear's picnic), and *Tribble Trouble;* the circus – has an influence on the form of the games which are often a montage of attractions with an emphasis on oddities and the bizarre; graffiti – in the game *Painter* you are armed with a spray can and realistic squirting noises; music –'popular' tunes such as 'High Noon' and 'The Yellow Rose of Texas' are one of the attractions of cowboy stories. There are also combinations of sources, for example, sport and science fiction merge in a game where you 'race your light cycle on the infamous grid'.

It has often been noted that the television screen blends together all the variety of material it transmits as 'television'. The games homogenise an even greater variety of sources, and yet there are some surprising absences from possible game ingredients. Most of the borrowings are from popular forms that appeal to boys – one might have expected some girls' comics to have been adopted. There are one or two games marketed as *Games for Girls,* but these are not adventures. One, for example, is a simple representation of horse-jumping, and another is remedial maths. It is interesting that popular children's adventure writers such as Enid Blyton or Arthur Ransome have not so far been adapted for the games market. Apart from copyright problems it is likely that the familiar settings, relationships between groups of children and happy endings, do not adapt easily to a model of today's single hero waging a personal battle against overwhelming odds. The games market seems only interested in the very deadly or the very silly. The silliness often takes the form of parody, emphasising the self-conscious newness of computer technology and its potential power to upset existing practices and systems.

The games industry does not emphasise its own autonomy, but relies on realising familiar elements of popular culture in its own specific form. It recirculates meanings in such a way that the meanings simply seem to have arisen from the spirit of the times. Its image is not that of an industry making products for passive consumers, but of a people's technology which encourages and enables participation by all who wish to participate. The process of production is well understood by most of the consumers. Listings for games are printed in many magazines and books, and sheets of instructions for writing your own games are available. In this way the games seem to give a certain materiality to discourses about progress towards a dynamic, interactive, networking, high-tech culture. But at least half of the population is not playing along – so it remains an old boys' network.

Scene

It is interesting that the two most popular ways of using a television set other than to watch broadcast programmes – playing video games through a computer, or pop videos through a videocassette recorder – both apparently break with television's traditional role as world-window, undemanding of attention, having an illusion of real time, allowing us ordered glimpses into other people's lives and always with the tantalising possibility that the camera's scanning eye may pick up some exciting live event such as somebody's death or an embassy siege, and connect our aerial to it. Unplug the aerial and the spell of this particular liveness is broken. But when the real world is cut off from the set, television lets us see into, even go into, entirely other, magical worlds, where normal orienting boundaries are transgressed or effaced. This does not mean that our engagement with all these worlds is not one of liveness. Rather, the actual performance required of us in the video game is like being permanently connected to broadcast television's exciting live event.

Although the way that games and pop videos construct their respective worlds is very different, both attempt some kind of totalising experience which demands our undivided attention, temporarily eclipsing all other worlds. I shall examine later how this fits into contemporary discourses of holism, and the experience is also akin to what Lévi-Strauss identified as the 'totalitarian ambition of the savage mind' in contrast to the scientific thinking which aimed to divide the difficulty into as many parts as were necessary in order to solve it. As the explosion in information and technology in the last few years has made the possibilities of division seen infinite, the difficulties incomprehensible, and solutions remote, the popular imagination appears to have taken flight either into worlds like those presented by the pop videos where signs not anchored to meaning seem to suggest and encompass everything,[1] or into model environments like those of the video games where systems still have their own limited and understandable – though strange – internal coherence.

That the totalising experience presented by games is one of the reasons for their popularity is argued particularly clearly in *Gaming – the Future's Language*,[2] a book on role-playing games which claims that linear language no longer gives us information in the most helpful way – that we need to be able to grasp a whole system in a way which descriptions of its parts and their inter-relationships can never give us, but which a model, as in a game, can more easily represent. It is possible to see this concept – of modelling as a whole system – at work alongside the narrative patterns in individual television programmes too. The kind of dramatisation often used by *World in Action* or *Horizon* to demonstrate an issue of current affairs or human concern would be an example of this. Rather than facts being presented in series, a whole situation is shown in action.

In terms of individual psychology the search for knowledge through an experience of wholeness can perhaps be explained by this passage from the *Writings* of Melanie Klein: 'My experience has shown me that the first object of (the) instinct for knowledge is the interior of the mother's body, which the child first of all regards as an object of oral gratification and then as the scene where intercourse between its parents takes place, and where in its phantasy the father's penis and the children are situated.'[3] In relation to oral gratifi-

cation, Beverle Houston has already proposed that the satisfaction promised by the broadcast output of television is the
promise of endless consumption: 'in its endles flow of text,
(television) suggests the first flow of nourishment in and
from the mother's body, evoking a moment when the emerging sexual drive is still closely linked to – propped on – the
life and death urgency of the feeding instinct.'[4] And she goes
on to suggest how television may link the mother's body
with the world's body for the viewer. Television's flow produces the idea that 'the text issues from an endless supply
that is sourceless, natural, inexhaustible, and co-extensive
with. . . as abundant, as plentiful as that which is already
available to the viewer – psychological reality itself'. If the
satisfaction which broadcast television offers is an apparently
endless supply of sustenance, video games seem to aim more
at satisfying the player's curiosity about the interior of the
body from which the supply – and the player himself – origi-
nates: 'At the same time as (the child) wants to force its way
into its mother's body in order to take possession of the
contents. . . it wants to know what is going on and what
things look like in there'.[5] Klein's usefulness to the study of
video games is her extensive work with children and particularly her analyses of play using toys and other small objects
as expressions of fantasies and experiences, and making the
representational content of the play more revealing. In
analysing the sexual development of boys, she found: '. . . the
displacement of everything tht is frightening and uncanny
onto the invisible inside of a woman's body'.[6] So if it can be
deduced from the video games's appeal to boys that these
games may represent a journey into the 'maternal cave', it is
not surprising to find that the environment down there is a
hostile one.

The settings of the adventure games developed from the
dungeons of role-playing games into two kinds of dystopia:
the unnatural and the natural system. The unnatural system
is perhaps the lesser threat, even though it includes such

nightmare spaces as the *Catacombs,* where a maze materialises as you wander around it searching for treasure and a food supply before you starve to death or are eliminated by a passing monster; or the *Tomb of Dracula* where you have to ward off Dracula with a number of silver stakes while you steal his treasure from one of the many vaults; or the underground cavern in which you have to seek and destory *The Orb* before it destroys the earth; or the spaceship *Snowball* with its cargo of deep-frozen humans, one of whom – you – is woken up to deal with an 'alien' situation which has developed in one of the 7,000 locations in the ship.

The other kind of dystopia, the natural or semi-natural system, can be set actually within the human body, such as the mouth *(Molar Maul)* or the bloodstream *(Fantastic Voyage)* but these are clinical and restrained adventures in comparison with the non-human natural environments of an island or a greenhouse or a pond. These are places which appear to be pleasant, harmonious self-regulating systems from the perspective of the passer-by, but in close-up reveal themselves to be red in the many teeth and claws that await your arrival on the scene. The blurb for *Savage Pond,* for example, explains that the tranquil waters of the village pond 'hide a world ruled by death and destruction – governed by the laws of nature. You play the part of a tadpole. . .'. The same kind of socialised biology can be seen in television nature programmes whose main function seems to be to show the savageness of the world without *us,* a savageness which, it seems to be implied, is just below the surface in 'man' too, and has to be controlled by civilisation. In video games it is cities which are good safe places which have to be defended, and the natural environment which is dangerous, evil and has to be escaped from. But what are we to make of this obsessively asserted difference between the civilised human world and the destructiveness of nature? One interpretation is that 'man' fears both his own destructiveness and a fantasised retaliation from the object of his destructive fantasies. Hence the obsessive anxiety with which he repeats the games, where the scene of the struggle is on a scale either so large ('you alone are left to defend the Galaxy') or so small ('you play the part of a tadpole') that the tragic and the comic merge into hysteria; fight it out in the womb.

Language

Tribble Trouble, Dinky Doo, Boog-a-Boo and *Super-Glooper* show that as far as marketing is concerned a playful, infantile, use of language is the name of the game. But although many names rely for their effect on the sound of words, there is no spoken language within the games. Sometimes a character may sing to you, as in *The Hobbit,* but this has no narrative power. The text communicates to the player only by writing, or by other-worldly sound effects, or by the movement of objects. The player communicates by typing in a telegraphic forms of language. For example, a compound sentence such as 'draw sword and kill dragon then get gold and leave' would be the utmost in sophistication to be expected. Very often the player's only response is to simply touch a key or type one work, such as 'look'.

Although games using natural language may develop when or if home computers are made more powerful, it seems not unlikely that part of the attraction of the current games is their lack of facility with language and their consequent use of a different mode of expression, in which objects replace words as a form of communication. Todorov, in exploring the theme of 'the self' in literature of the fantastic, has noted what he calls 'a collapse of the limits between matter and mind' which is found also in madness, in drug experience and 'oddly enough', he says, 'in infants'.[7] As an example he illustrates the way that fantastic action often begins with figurative language: 'He curled himself into a ball and the ball rolled from room to room'. Melanie Klein notes: 'In its play, the child acts instead of speaking. It puts actions –

which originally took the place of thoughts – in the place of words'.[8]

Although the players of video games are generally older than infants and not usually mad or on drugs, it seems that in certain situations, for example in the transference situation of psychoanalysis and in some kinds of games, infantile emotions and fantasies can easily be revived: '. . . I found it of great value from the clinical and theoretical point of view that I was analysing both adults and children. I was thereby able to observe the infant's phantasies and anxieties still operative in the adult'.[9] In the games, the magical value of objects often comes from the way they represent something which is usually expressed in language. For example – you are in a dark cave, the light you are carrying suddenly goes out and you are told that something slimy is encircling your legs. You type the command 'look' and are told that you see an octopus grasping your leg with its many tentacles ('hands'). Do you pick it up, or do you kill it? Your dilemma could be illuminated by your knowledge of the expression 'many hands make light work'.

Even objects assumed to be inert matter can and in many cases do, take on the qualities of life – a sword may pick itself up off the floor and put itself in your hand. And you can always use any object as a form of communication by hurling it at the addressee.

Quest

Most of the adventure games involve some sort of quest, but because the narrative coincides absolutely with the action, since the reader has become a a performer, the usual structure of the quest, and indeed of narrative, is disturbed. Apart from the different position of the reader/performer the narratives resemble those of the exotic thriller, the travel story or science fiction or, more usually, a combination of all three, with a dash of the uncanny as well. Klein found that in the

genres of story that particularly appealed to boys, there was
also an emphasis on technology:

In many analyses of boys of the pre-pubertal period or sometimes
even in the latency period most of the time is taken up with stories
about Red Indians or with detective stories or with phantasies
about travel, adventures and fighting, told in serial form and often
associated with descriptions of imaginary technical inventions,
such as special kinds of boats, machines, cars contrivances used in
warfare, and so on.[10]

She does not discuss the symbolism of the technical inventions, which is surprising considering the part they often
play in male quests, but she does emphasise that the fantasy
stories are about a search for knowledge in whic organs of
perception, tools of penetration and, presumably, means of
transport can become equated with each other:

By means of the penetrating penis which is equated with an organ
of perception, to be more precise, with the eye, the ear or a combination of the two (the boy) wants to discover what sort of
destruction has been done inside his mother by his own penis and
excrements and by his father's and to what kind of perils his penis
is exposed here.[11]

The same equation seems to exist in the different levels
involved in playing video games, where the performer is
using the technology of the computer keyboard to transport
a character who represents his own perceptions round a space
which represents his mother's body to discover its dangers
and to take away the treasures which it contains: 'The Knight's
Quest – the idea of this game is to guide a knight, who is
your eyes and ears, around the country looking for the lost
treasures of Merlin'.[12] Most stories begin with a lack which
involves the hero going somewhere. But whereas 'quest' narratives have generally been concerned primarily with the
hero's departure, his leaving home – and have often been
interpreted as the adolescent male's process of separating

himself from the family to find 'himself' elsewhere – in the games it is clear that the movement 'away from' stands in for a repressed 'movement towards' the mother's body. It has been pointed out that the irony of Oedipus's situation was that his journey was a return to his family trouble and not a movement away from it as he had thought.

If most quest stories are about a search for knowledge of the interior of the mother's body and the nourishment it contains, then there are at least two different objects of the quest: one at the level of the search for knowledge and one at the level of the fiction, which is an actual object such as lost treasures, or the Holy Grail. In most non-game stories the eventual finding of the actual object satisfies us as readers because it usually coincides with a resolution of all strands of the plot, and because we can identify with the hero's enjoyment of, for example, 'the nourishment of the Holy Grail (which) feeds the soul even as it sustains the body'.[13] In a game, however, we do not identify with someone else's satisfaction, we expect to experience it. So finding the actual object of the quest is invariably disappointing, except in the game which contained clues as to the whereabouts of real buried treasure, but then the satisfaction was outside of the game.

Since there can be no adequate reward for success the game has to be about lack itself – the desire to continue to play – rather than about a final satisfying resolution. Although there is a basic cause-effect structure, the enigmas that keep you playing are not to do with what the treasure will be like, but rather what the next environment will be like, and what will happen there. The events or adventures themselves do not seem to be related to each other by anything but time and place. The environment is important as a container of a variety of hazards – so description in the games is always part of the action – but the hazards do not have any logical connection with each other. For example, you may be in a room with two doors, one guarded by a monster and one unguarded. If you choose to avoid the monster and try to leave by the other door it may open onto a chute which drops you down five floors into a room which could be nearer or further from your destination and will contain it own set of hazards. There are no moral principles such as reward for taking the difficult path or facing up to problems. Obstacles are there only to reinforce desire. The performer is a believer in chance operations and the games progress by the mechanism of surprise rather than suspense, which is also characteristic of uncanny or 'marvellous' narratives in other media.

Unlike other quest narratives the games rarely end with a triumphant and heroic return. This is partly because the hero is not entirely heroic. His behaviour is often like that of a thief. If he gets away at all his return is an undignified flight, and there is rarely anyone to marry to round things off. Women are not there as rewards, they are the landscape, the scene in which the performance takes place. The fascination of video games is not related to resolution; rather it is to be looked for in the opportunites provided for repetition of a set of actions, performed with an almost neurotic compulsion.

Performer

One of the agreed criteria for evaluating a video game is its level of addictiveness. No doubt this is also a criterion among television programme controllers for evaluating series and serials, but in no other cultural form is repeatability of exactly the same experience given such explicit value as it is in games. It seems likely that the addiction is related to the fact that the person who plays the game has some physical participation in it, even if, or because, only at arm's length. It seems important to investigate the fascination of this repetition, not least because, according to some 'purist' accounts, one of the characteristics of popular culture has always been an element of participation, with a resulting awkwardness of the relation between narratives and popular culture. Perhaps the games, crossing the borderlines between story-telling and participatory sport, may be setting a new style for popular narrative.

In the games, 'audience' disappears as the distinction between 'doer' and 'viewer'. The viewer is in a separate space but appears to be in the position of co-creator, or subject to which everything else is the predicate. And yet the emphasis, or at least all the interest, is in that predicate, the paranoiac environment. The performer himself has no character traits that are not causal – because he is adventurous, he has an adventure – and, needless to say, there is no development of character as the game progresses. It is the game that controls, as the 'dungeon master' or 'Destinateur', with the performer as only a function of its flow. You perform in it. It performs for you. It performs you. So the enigmas for the performer are of the order of 'where am I?' rather than 'who am I?'. The performer is also apparently a double or a split subject since the game is simultaneously in the first person (you in the real world pressing keys), and the third person (a character on the screen, such as a knight, who represents you in the world of the fiction). This is a different kind of split from that in a spectator watching a film, for example, where identifications can be with a variety of characters and positions. For the performer of a game the first and third person are almost totally identified, so there can be no suspense based on knowing more (having seen more) than the protagonist who represents you. 'Protagonist' is perhaps an inappropriate description since, as the function of the flow, the performer reacts rather than acts.

In the description of most games it is made clear that the performer is on the defensive: he is defending either the entire universe, or Watford or himself-as-tadpole, against destructive forces. Also clear, though sometimes contradictory, is that a kamikaze motivation is the rule rather than the exception. In arcade games you expect to be attacked by sheets of kamikaze aliens, but in the adventure games it is your own behaviour that is suicidal. This is frequently made explicit in the names of games and their software houses, for example, *Get Liquidated*, Kamikaze, Terminal Software. The unlikelihood of your survival seems in fact to be a criterion of a 'good' game, part of its addictiveness. It is quite frightening to try to give an explanation for the popularity of suicide, an explanation which must be in terms of a complex interweaving of many elements. But in relation to the games, however, these elements seem to include a reaction to the threat of nuclear war, a reactivation of infantile feelings triggered by the games, and partly, perhaps, the attractions of masochism. Masochism puts you, as the object of other people's sadistic or murderous intentions, at the centre of attention, which goes some way to shift the emphasis of the game away from the predicate and back to yourself as subject.

Having a nothing-left-to-lose position also overrides the necessity for you to have any other positions, values or ideas and so concentrates your mind on crisis management – a social skill not without its value in Britain in the 1980s. The crises are always *now*, in real-time, live. There are no flashbacks or flashforwards. The game is attached to the present and to reality through the person of the performer. But the first-person performer who presses the keys is actually also in liminal time. Within the game's time there is a close relationship between time and language. All language is performative, and there is no taking refuge in silence. Most situations have to be responded to immediately or they are overtaken by nasty events. This affects the player's time in the real world. Continuing to perform in the game, as in *TheArabian Nights,* is the same as continuing to live. When you stop you die, and the narrative stops too. You have no perspective from which to watch it to the end, you can only presume that the equilibrium reasserts itself, having expelled you.

So what is the pleasure in the repetition of this life and death performance? Melanie Klein argues that what causes the repetition compulsion in children's play is anxiety about an unreal danger directed towards the insides of their own bodies. We are concerned here not with how this anxiety arises, but how it is dealt with. In this, Melanie Klein's theory is informed by her practice in analysing children and her success in relieving their anxiety. According to her theory each sex has its own essentially different mode of 'mastering' anxiety. The boy, putting all his faith in the omnipotence of his penis-as-magic-wand (not surprising in a culture which values this object so highly) turns the danger from an internal to an external one and 'embodies' it as his father's penis inside his mother's body. The strategy is to go into battle with a similar weapon to that of the enemy, and in a theatre of war well away from his own insides.[14] Once having entered the mother's body in fantasy he risk the danger of being castrated by his father's penis, which is waiting for him in there, or of having his own penis prevented from retreating, and being shut inside his mother's body:

These phantasies contain such ideas that 'the penis incorporated into the mother, turns into a dangerous animal or into weapons loaded with explosive substances'; or that her vagina, too, is transformed into an instrument of death, as for instance, a poisoned mouse-trap.[15]

However, if he performs well he will be able to destroy everything in sight and escape intact. After this he is often overwhelmed by a need to restore what he has destroyed, but doubts his ability to do this:

His fear of not being able to put things right again arouses his still deeper fear of being exposed to the revenge of the objects which, in his phantasy, he has killed and which keep on coming back again. . . it is not until a rather more advanced stage has been reached that its anxiety is also felt as a sense of guilt and sets the obsessional mechanisms in motion. One is amazed to discover that. . . the mastering of anxiety has become (the child's) greatest pleasure.[16]

But, of course, the anxiety can never be finally mastered by this mechanism.

The endeavour in this account is to show the centrality of the relationship of the infant to the mother's body; the fact that this is so clear in video games, is, I think, more important than the boy's use of the phallus-penis as a means of separating himself from his mother. Since, I believe, 'the masculine position' has not changed much since Melanie Klein was analysing her little boys crashing engines and cars together (and the male directors of silent films were putting the same scenes on the screen) it would be surprising if boys adopted any other mechanism for separating, and even more amazing if they were able to repudiate separation itself. Although it can be argued that society is (however slowly) beginning to de-centre men – through changing work patterns as much as through changing discoures of sexuality – it is still no surprise that men respond to this uncertainty by inventing things that, while seeming new, while seeming to offer a breakdown of boundaries, help them master anxiety by re-asserting the old boundaries and differences.

Machine

As demonstrated by Melanie Klein's observations, and cultural forms such as the James Bond phenomenon, machinery seems to be a necessary part of male fantasy and performance. The camera that Vertov thought he was, seemed to offer a precision that humans could only envy and aspire to. The new generation of machines produces an even more ecstatic identification, for they offer a magical liberation from all kinds of rigidity, including the laws of time and space. Video games can use computer graphics to produce multi-perspec-tival representations, a fourth dimension, making our normal perceptions of time and space seem inadequate. Video-effects technology, now widespread in the commercials and music industries, seduces the viewer into identifying with an un-defined future – represented by laser-light and processed sound – which has a relationship which needs to be explored with a present which is in some ways over-defined, and in other ways falling apart.

Not only has technology been incorporated into art, but the performance of a machine, like that of a person, is now no longer judged by what objects it can make, but what it can organise, what effects it can create. The structure of pre-sent technology is less important in the popular imagination than the more visible structure of the old mechanical machines were in their day. There is little fun in taking an integrated circuit apart, so the emphasis is now on the process of working with the machines rather than on understanding how they work. Behind all of which is the frightening fact that the machines of artificial intelligence are incomprehen-sible to the people who work with them, are out of touch with human reality, and therefore are, to all intents and pur-poses, out of control.

This power that the new technology is rightly feared to have may partly account for the carefully cultivated 'cuddly' image of the micro-computer. Posters selling them to the business world often use childlike motifs, such as cartoon figures from children's television programmes, to show how simple they are. Publicity for the video games themselves is usually so extreme in its death-and-destruciton imagery that its obvious parody undercuts the fear. Some games incorp-orate an element of bathos: 'Find and destroy the Dictator's battle headquarters and save Watford'; and sometimes the scale of a game is that of a micro-world in which the pro-tagonist is a tadpole, or a flea. All of which builds on the unspoken fear that the future of the world is indeed with the machines of artificial intelligence and if you can't lick 'em. . . .

Women and fantasy

Feminist work has begun to enter debates about popular culture through studies of cultural forms which are popular with women, such as the 'woman's film' of 1940s cinema or television soap operas. This is a welcome complement to the emphasis on male pleasures given by studies of sport and crime fiction, but it still begs the question of why there should be such a clearly marked split along gender lines in popular cultural forms. This section tentatively suggests some psychoanalytical and cultural reasons why women's fantasies are different from men's and lead to a different kind of cultural activity.

The position of women has changed considerably since Melanie Klein's *Writings,* so it seems appropriate to augment her work here with observations and theory from more recent feminist psychoanalytical practice, and I have particularly drawn on that of Luise Eichenbaum and Susie Orbach at the Women's Therapy Centre in London. Both Klein and the more recent studies suggest that girls come to terms with their earliest anxiety in a different way from boys. The anxiety is still about an unreal threat to their insides, which in boys in our culture gets confused with anxiety about their different anatomy from that of the mother and their consequent need to separate, with the result that the boy projects his fear onto the mother's body and fights the Oedipal conflict in there with his penis. In girls the original anxiety is not overlaid by anxiety about differences, so the threat is not projected outwards and remains a threat to their insides. Klein suggests that the girl feels that her body is poisoned and for this reason needs good nourishment from the mother's body to make it well again. The observations at the Women's Therapy Centre also suggest that girls' and women's feelings of lack are usually about the need for nourishment. The therapists make clear that this in their view is in opposition to the penis-envy theory: 'We have found no evidence that the way women experience themselves as inadequate connects in any way with the fantasy of a penis or its transformation into a baby'.[17]

The frustration the girl suffers at never being able to get enough nourishment leads, according to Klein, to fantasy attacks on the mother's body using as weapons the faeces (represented by shiny things) and magical thoughts. But the mother's body, because of the anatomical identity with her own, which it also represents, is an uncomfortable setting for a war game, so in the girl's fantasy the emphasis is not on the attack but rather on the need to repair the damage the attacks have done. For women, then, the leading anxiety, obsession and therefore pleasure is about restitution. Melanie Klein notes that girls will pile up pieces of paper neatly in a box until it is quite full. The neatness and carefulness are because restitutive acts must adhere in every detail to the damage done in fantasy. She observed that drawing, sewing, making dolls' dresses or reading books were typical ways of reconstituting the mother's body, and thereafore the girl's own. She maintains that giving birth to a baby is particularly satisfying because it signifies that the interior of the woman's body is unharmed and can produce good things, which in fantasy represents restoring a number of objects, even in some cases recreating a whole world.

Although it is not possible here to go into detail, it is important to note that Eichenbaum and Orbach argue very strongly that women's anxiety and their specific ways of dealing with it are culturally and historically produced and are mediated through the psychology of the mother and the effect of the social position of women on the mother's psychology. There is also nothing in Melanie Klein's observations – as opposed to her arguments – that suggests a biological essentialism about the way the two sexes deal with anxieties. She noted that girls do make attacks, and are not lacking in weapons when necessary. Similarly, boys do have a restitutive phase after an attack and will often build towns and villages with the toys. The implication is therefore that the pressures which produce and maintain a gendered split between activities of attack and those of restitution are cultural. The activities themselves then become part of the pressures which discourage women from projecting outwards and fighting for what they need, and which prevent men form recognising their restitutive needs except in sublimations such as do-it-yourself.

The obsessions in both sexes seem to start in response to a cultural pressure for separation. It has always been assumed that separation from the mother was more difficult for boys than for girls, because of the complication of the Oedipus conflict, but Eichenbaum and Orbach maintain that in fact separation is easier for the male gender because the anatomical differences make boundaries clearer. This may suggest that a fixed sexual identity is also easier for, and more important to, men since they are defining themselves *against* something. Later men then try to define women against their male otherness, but because women did not begin by defining themselves in difference, they may be less phobic about undefined sexuality, and this has implications for their preferred cultural forms.

Since our culture is dominated by male definitions of women, it is not surprising that in their most popular forms women's fantasies appear in the guise of romances or soap operas, where the preoccupation is with reconciliation – or lack of it – in relationships. However, it is quite instructive to look at the more conscious fantasies of feminist fiction where women are renegotiating their identity. The most striking feature of these in the context of the above discussion is the emphasis placed on new worlds, often Utopian, or on new creatures with different or unclear sex/gender boundaries. But also interesting is the fact that if Greimas's model of the quest narrative is placed over these feminist narratives there are large passages which fall outside the model – usually passages in which nothing happens. This exercise also reveals that many of the narratives are reverse quests, often away from male culture, which is represented by civilisation and high technology, and towards the 'womb of nature', and either a primitive, artisanal culture, or complete distintegration.[18]

So, it is not surprising that video games and other forms of popular interest based on battles have little appeal for women. Video games are particularly unattractive since they are part of a technology which (unfortunately, in my view) is identified with male power, and they are about mastering a specifically male anxiety in a specifically male way. The obsessive activities of restoration which are performable, and have been in continuous performance by women for hundreds of years, such as knitting, sewing, looking after and talking about babies, similarly seem to have little appeal for men. It is perhaps for this reason that they have never been studied seriously as part of popular culture. So far men's need to project has led to their obsessions being amplified and made available to us all. It would take major cultural and material changes to shift the emphasis on to activities of restoration and this is perhaps partly why the separate development of a low-tech culture seems so appealing to many women at the present time. It seems to be the only opposition, however unrealistic.

Conclusion

We must make allowance for the complex and unstable process whereby discourse can be both an instrument and an effect of power, but also a hindrance, a stumbling-block, a point of resistance and a starting point for an opposing strategy.
  Michel Foucault, *The History of Sexuality*, Vol. 1, p. 101.

In trying to understand the relationship between gender and the micro-world of video games the discourse of psychoanalysis has been a helpful one, but in order now to look at the place of the games within the wider relationships between gender, technology, history and cultural forms, other discourses have to be brought in. The statement of Foucault which introduces this section suggests a framework for looking at this interrelationship of discourses. It is fairly clear how discourse can be an instrument of power, but less obvious how it comes to be a point of resistance. Foucault proposes the idea of 'reverse' discourses. He demonstrates that a discourse which projects and amplifies itself enough also makes it possible for a reverse discourse to be formed and heard from the place which it addresses. A reverse discourse is not necessarily an oppositional one since it is constructed in the terms of the one that brought it into being, but it can be the starting point for an opposing strategy. So, for example, the nineteenth-century discourse which integrated the woman's body into the sphere of medical practice eventually produced a reverse discourse from women about their rights over their own bodies. This has helped women gain some control over their own fertility and sexuality, but it has also kept women's discourse preoccupied with the body and with sexuality, until recently, when the concern with body over individual reproduction and life has grown into an opposition to the technologies of mass destruction and, by extension, has reinforced an opposition to all technology. A recognition that the technologies of war are related to male anxieties and desires is summed up in the anti-nuclear slogan 'take the toys from the boys'.

The focus on the body, however, has also generated a discourse about wholeness – coming no doubt as well from women's anxieties about restitution – which has emphasised the integration of all systems of the body and denied separations between psychic and physical states. This has fed into already existing discourses about alternatives to western medicine, and indeed to western science and philosophy. So there is now a growing popular discourse of 'holism' which, if not re-instating an Aristotelian universe or Lévi-Strauss's 'savage mind', is certainly supporting religious intuitive thinking as against scientific ways of understanding. This discourse can be seen at work in the totalising represenations of both the utopias of feminist fiction and the dystopias of video games. It also partly explains the blurring of border-lines, in both forms, between past, present and future. It is impossible to totalise the jumble of the present unless it is seen as the future of something past or 'the past of something yet to come',[19] or unless our brains could hold, process and access as much information as a powerful computer, and as rapidly. There is a fear, a fearful knowledge, which is scarcely to be recognised as real, that we are entering a time when a great deal of executive power will be realised through, if not transferred to, machines. Power will become unassailable, because invisible. With this knowledge of power come anxieties about exploitation and manipulation, about inabil-ity to separate oneself from it. To this fear video games are in many ways the predictable male response: the video screen makes the fear visible, but obliquely, for like the Medusa, it must not be directly confronted; the visibility of the fear allows it to be expressed but remain unspoken; the quest for the performer's destiny occupies the fantasy space in which infantile battles were fought in the mother's body and won; the male references in the intertextualty of the content of the games gives the male player a sense of familiarity which helps him over the strangeness of the new technology; the domestic image and setting of the home computer constantly remind the performer of his mastery and his power to switch the machine off, even if it does beat him at his own game. And as his own game seems to be the rehearsing of his own death, to lose is only to affirm his own resurrection. Foucault points out the irony that the forces which have power over life, now translated into the management of survival because of their capability of producing death on a global scale, can only be avoided by the individual's right to suicide. All

aspects of life, particularly sexuality, being so closely scrutin-
ised, death remains the only secret. However, as it is only in
the fantasy of the video games that a single suicidal enemy
is a real threat to a strong power, there seems little potential for
a discourse from the position of death becoming an oppositional force to be reckoned with. On the evidence of the
games the preferred male solution seems to be to bury themselves in the mother's body with their fantasy weapons and
forget about the very real dangers in the world outside until
these dangers manifest themselves as disputes about boundaries, as in the Falklands 'crisis', in which case they can be
understood and dealt with by playing the war game, again.

If there is the possibility of a reverse discourse to the one
that aligns the uses of technology with maleness, with domination and eventually with destruction, it has to come from
the position where technology and women are addressed as
the same thing, or as part of the same scenario, and has to
take account of the part technology plays in male fantasy.
While technology is seen as weapons to be used in the hellish
battles within women's bodies, women will never be seen, or
be able to see themselves as the users of technology: 'In the
micro industry 99·9 per cent of customers are men, largely
because the product is beyond the cerebral capacity of the
weaker sex and also because it doesn't come in pretty colours'.

It is not of course just infantile fantasies that sustain opinions like that, found in the magazine *Computer Dealer*. Such
opinions are supported by other discourses, but particularly
those relating to sexualty.

Foucault believed that in the nineteenth century sexuality
was constructed and used as one of the technologies of
power, as power changed from being the power to inflict
death to the power to manage and organise life and survival.
I would argue that sexuality is now such an important form
of control and so implicated in discourses of power and domination that technology itself has had to become sexualised
in order for it to be apparently under control.

There is already a growing concern among educators about the lack of participation by women in the new technology, but so far this concern has only manifested itself in terms of an 'equal opportunities' issue. In order to help a reverse discourse to emerge, more work needs to be done on the relationship between a technologised sexuality and a sexualised technology.

Notes

1 E. Ann Kaplan, 'A postmodern play of the signifier? MTV advertising, pastiche, and schizophrenia', paper given to the International Television Studies' Conference, London, 1984.

2 R. D. Duke, Gaming – the Future's Language (London: Sage, 1974).

3 Melanie Klein, Writings, II (London: Hogarth Press, 1980) pp. 173-4.

4 Beverle Houston, 'Viewing television: the metapsychology of endless consumption', paper given to ITSC, London, 1984.

5 Klein, op. cit., p. 174.

6 Ibid., p. 260.

7 T. Todorov, The Fantastic (New York: Cornell, 1975), p. 115.

8 Klein, op. cit., p. 9.

9 Klein, Writings, III, p. 138.

10 Klein, Writings, II, p. 81n.

11 Ibid., p. 245.

12 R. Bilboul, J. Durrant and M. Spencer, The Good Software Guide (London: Fontana, 1984), p. 25.

13 The Holy Grail, quoted in T. Todorov, The Poetics of Prose, (Oxford: Blackwell, 1977) (note the association with Mothering!).

14 Ronald Reagan's proposal for a real live performance of Star Wars seems to be based on the same strategy.

15 Klein, op. cit., II, p. 132.

16 Ibid., p. 169.

17 Luise Eichenbaum and Susie Orbach, Understanding Women, (London: Pelican, 1985), p. 31n. 10.

18 For this information I am grateful to a workshop on The uses and applications of Greimas' model for the analysis of novels written by women, led by Kristien Hemmerechts at the Women's Writing Conference held at Manchester Polytechnic in September 1984. Greimas' model can be read in A. J. Greimas, Semantique Structurale (Paris: Larousse, 1966); and Du Sens (Paris: Seuil, 1970). There is an English translation/adaptation of these models given in J. Culler, Structuralist Poetics, (London: Routledge and Kegan Paul, 1975). The novels studied in relation to the model were: M. Atwood, Surfacing; D. Lehmann, Dusty Answer; J. Rhys, Good Morning Midnight; M. Sinclair, Life and Death of Harriet Frean; and S. Townsend Warner, Lolly Willowes.

19 F. Jameson, 'Progress versus Utopia, or can we imagine the future?' in Science Fiction Studies 9, 1982.

Popular culture:
practice and institution

A number of attempts have been made in recent years to map the field of studies of 'popular culture'. In view of the apparent impossibility of ever arriving at a single definition of this term, theoretical attention has shifted to the 'problematics' within which 'popular culture' circulates. Articles have appeared outlining two problematics ('culturalism' and 'structuralism'), or even three, (these two, plus classical Marxism) within the terrain of cultural studies,[1] and much speculation has been directed at a possible synthesis of these various theoretical traditions. The Open University course U203 Popular Culture, for example, in its theoretical discourse, maps out the dichotomy of two problematics and posits the Gramscian concept of 'hegemony' as providing a bridge between them.[2] In this now familiar formulation, popular culture is located in a site of struggle between so-called 'lived cultures' (the preserve of 'culturalism') and 'dominant ideology' (the object of 'structuralist Marxism', as defined, for example, in Althusser's essay).[3]

It is not my intention, in this chapter, to initiate a critique of these theoretical formulations. Rather, I want to develop a couple of thoughts regarding their institutional conditions; that is to say, I want to look at the *practice* of cultural studies in this period of theoretical definition. The question I want to raise is this: what were the impulses behind these attempts at mapping the field of popular culture? What was happening to cultural studies in this period? I shall focus my attention on the two institutions whose position in this field seems to have been pivotal, namely the Open University Course, and the work of the Centre for Contemporary Cultural Studies at Birmingham.

Now there seems to be a fairly conventional account of the development of cultural studies during the past decade – an account which has become the 'common sense' of some researchers in this field. This is an account which emphasises a shift in academic practice, due to a number of transformations in the institutional conditions of work. Putting it crudely perhaps, cultural studies has been 'professionalised', and here U203 is only the most visible sign of a general tendency. In a recent review of the field, Richard Johnson refers to this as a tendency to 'academic codification' as research gets taught, and as a continuous theoretical tradition is defined.[4] He expresses some reservations about these developments:

Cultural studies is now a widely taught subject, especially in tertiary education, though not always under this name. Unless we are very careful students will encounter it as an orthodoxy, especially, perhaps, where teacher attachments to the subject are pragmatic. In any case, students now have lectures, courses and examinations in the study of culture. In these circumstances, how can they occupy a critical tradition critically?[5]

A familiar position is articulated here – a position which revolves around the opposition between 'critical work' and 'orthodoxy'. In this account the 'pressure to define' the field, to map out its problematics, is explained by the necessity to occupy institutional spaces (in tertiary education). However, within this 'pressure' something is in danger of being lost: an original critical spirit of cultural studies, the sense of a collective project, of an intervention within traditional academic disciplines. The burden of Richard Johnson's argument is that this sense of critical work should be maintained. He is sceptical of the value of 'academic codification', and deeply worried by 'the disconnection that occurs when cultural studies is inhabited for merely academic purposes'.[6] In short, there is a danger here of a sell-out of the radical and interventionist 'political-intellectual stance' that gave rise to cultural studies.

Now I have characterised this as a familiar and conventional argument. It is familiar of course, in other areas of political and cultural work: the sense of an 'original moment' subsequently compromised by institutional pressures. However, although the argument is familiar, there are some points which it articulates that do require attention. There may well be a tendency to 'academic codification', for instance, as teaching involves a certain repetition of debates and texts, and perhaps a pressure to be less eclectic. At another level it is clear that a profound shift occurs in the conditions of work imposed by conventional academic practice. A potential casualty here is the notion of 'collective work', of group research and debate, which has been a major achievement both at the Birmingham Centre and at the Open University. These difficulties are compounded by the practice of 'distance learning' at the O U – a problem which is highlighted in the concluding section of U203, and confronted, to some extent, at summer schools. Nevertheless there are pressures here towards definition and perhaps towards orthodoxy. The question is, does this amount to a compromise, or even a sell-out, of a radical intellectual tradition?

I think there are reasons to question this kind of formulation, this way of putting it. As I have suggested, this is not to ignore the real problems that have to be confronted, for example in devising an Open University course – nor is it to deny the very real achievement which is represented by U203. But it is to question the 'commonsense' tendency to interpret these developments as a sign of compromise. On one level, it is too facile to represent 'codification' in Richard

Johnson's terms, as 'systematic closure'.[7] An argument could be made, I think, in favour of a more 'disciplined', less eclectic, approach to popular culture – if we are clear about the 'disciplines' involved. But as a way into this argument I should first like to address the assumption that a potential 'loss' is involved. As I have suggested, this is based on the invocation of a 'critical' cultural studies tradition.

Essentially, my approach at this point will be to question the nature of that 'tradition'. It is too easily assumed I think, that cultural studies represented, in its foundation, a radical intervention in academic institutions. At least, the nature of that intervention should be clearly defined. One way of defining it is to inquire into the 'discursive formation' of cultural studies: that is, to interrogate what the practice of cultural studies has involved. In other words, this is not to attempt to define the term 'popular culture', nor indeed to map the field of its problematics – rather, it is to ask what the concept of 'popular culture' has *produced*. What has it meant to take this as an object of study; what discourses and methods of study have been available; what *kinds* of 'political-intellectual stance' have been taken? In this chapter I can do no more than scratch the surface of this formation, but I do think that an 'archaeology' of the discourses of cultural studies might begin to problematise the assumption of a radical tradition.

So what kinds of discursive practice are available in cultural studies? I have taken two passages – one from U203, the second from the Birmingham Centre – which seem to me to illustrate two principal positions in the study of popular culture. These are <u>not</u>, I must emphasise, theoretical positions – they are *discursive* positions: that is, positions from which certain kinds of writing are produced, enabling the circulation of certain kinds of statements. In fact, a good deal of effort has gone into reconciling these statements at a theoretical level; it is only when you examine their 'discursivity' that a divergence becomes apparent. And it seems to me that despite their different institutional locations (at the Open University, and at the Birmingham Centre) there are some deep continuities to be traced in these discourses.

My first passage comes from the concluding unit of U203 (Block 7, Unit 32). One paragraph constitutes an entire subsection:

4 Incursions

Dick Hebdige's article on taste focused on what was, in effect, a crisis period for our culture. A period in which many of the old certainties began to crumble and fade away. A time in which the official language of culture could no longer be accepted as uniform and univocal (who can now listen to John Snagge, Bob Danvers-Walker or the earnestness of those newsreels without an ironic smile on their face evoked by the uncynical confidence of their tones?). New and particular languages have emerged – the language of working-class subcultures, the languages of the English regions, more dramatically perhaps the languages of the Celtic nationalisms – all registering a profound crisis in national, linguistic and symbolic identity. The post-war settlement is now in ruins, its consensus to be reconstructed by the emergence of a 'third force' in British politics. New sites of struggle have emerged over the past twenty years, and particularly those of race and gender: blacks and women are involved in a fight not only for better 'conditions' but also in the process of *finding a voice* which, as the voice of Linton Kwesi Johnson showed in Unit 29, would not necessarily sound harmonious to English ears. The Women's Movement, in turn, has done much politically, culturally and theoretically to overturn many deeply embedded tastes and values in our common culture. Now, more than ever perhaps in recent history, the cultural field is fraught with contradictions and sensing threats to its unity. Neither the dominant image of the nation, nor the national culture, nor national unity can be restored except, as the Falklands adventure has shown, by recourse to essentially pre-war ideas and archaic linguistic forms. Something quite substantial has happened to the British culltural field: something that has shifted many of its recognisable landmarks and displaced may of its lines of force.[8]

What is going on in this example? Does it seem strange that such a piece of writing should appear in the conclusion to this course? Clearly, the strategy seems to be to make the course relevant to a sense of the present, to the 'current situation'. Is this the 'political-intellectual stance' which Richard Johnson locates in the foundation of cultural studies? If so, we can observe that a particular kind of stance is adopted here. From the perspective offered by the course, the student is invited to survey the 'cultural field', as it is defined. Diverse sites of struggle (blacks, women, Celtic nationalisms) and historical events (the Falklands) are all drawn into a totality ('our culture') in a particular conjuncture (the 'crisis period').

I would characterise this as a discourse of social commentary. It has a distinct pedigree in the study of popular culture, and may be traced at least as far as the work of Matthew Arnold, and other nineteenth-century critics. In the left inflection of this discourse, the culture/anarchy dichotomy is rewritten as a narrative of 'culture in crisis', but otherwise its totalising strategy is the same.[9] Diverse cultural developments are interpreted as a 'sign of the times', or of the 'state of the nation'. The narrative unifies these developments around its sign of 'crisis', and allows for an element of political diagnosis and speculation. In all this, a rhetorical appeal is made to the reader's recognition ('who can now listen. . .', etc.) – a reader who is already placed within this narrative, whose experience bears out the truth of its predictions. In short, this is the discourse of the literary essay, a kind of superior journalism. Within its terms the intellectual can make particular kinds of 'political' moves: from the study of culture, to the pages of *New Socialist* or *Marxism Today*.

Alongside social commentary, there is another quite distinctive discursive position in the study of popular culture:

The rigorous stage of the analysis, the elimination of distortion, the cross-checking of evidence and so on have served to focus points of divergence and convergence between systems. Reducing the confusion of the research situation, providing a more precise orientation for analysis, allows a closer reading of separate realities. By reading moments of contact and divergence it becomes possible to delineate other worlds, demonstrating their inner symbolic qualities. And when the conventional techniques retire, when they cannot follow the subjects of subjects themselves – this is the moment of *reflexivity*. Why are these things happening? Why has the subject behaved in this way? Why do certain areas remain obscure to the researcher? What differences in orientation lie behind the failure to communicate?

It is here, in this interlocking of human meanings, of cultural codes and of forms, that there is the possibility of 'being surprised'. And in terms of the generation of 'new' knowledge, we know what it is precisely *not* because we have shared it – the usual notion of empathy – but because we have *not* shared it. It is here that the classical canons are overturned. It is time to ask and explore, to discover the differences between subjective positions, between cultural forms. It is time to initiate actions or to break expectations in order to probe different angles in different lights. Of course, this is a time of maximum disturbance to researchers, whose own meanings are being thoroughly contested. It is precisely at this point that the researcher must assume an unrestrained and hazardous *self-reflexivity*. And it is the turning away from a full commitment, at this point, which finally limits the methods of traditional sociology.[10]

Ethnography has become a key method in cultural analysis, and here Paul Willis specifies its 'political-intellectual stance'. It is important to note the shift from a naturalistic representation of exotic cultures, to a reflexive concentration on the research encounter itself. In this encounter the research paradigm is 'surprised' and even 'disturbed', with the subjective position of the researcher implicated in the disturbance. Significantly, Willis also proceeds to characterise these encounters as 'moments of crisis'. What distinguishes cultural studies from traditional sociology is its commitment to seeing them through.

The discourse of ethnography in cultural studies can be located at the limits of a practice of social inquiry. This is another nineteenth-century inheritance, with its origins in superior journalism – in particular, the work of Henry Mayhew.[11] At first sight, the position taken here seems quite

different from that assumed by the essayist: a located commitment, rather than a magisterial overview. But there are deep
continuities between these formulations. Once again 'culture' is located at a site of 'crisis', a threat posed by the mysterious 'other world'. Once again, this is a threat to an
assumed position, a common culture, as 'we' are surprised
by the disturbance. To be sure, the left intellectual does not
simply gaze on the exotic as an object of anthropological
fascination; nor, even though he does speak of 'theoretical
confession', is Willis's account reducible to a crisis of consci-
ence. On the contrary, it is a site for 'further theorisation';
but it is not unknown for this theory to deliver its troubled
subject – via a series of 'mediations' – precisely to a narrative
of 'crisis' in the culture as a whole.[12]

It would be tempting, but excessive, to suggest that this
constitutes a unified discursive formation. Tempting:
because it might be argued that ethnography provides the
characters and settings for a familiar plot, and practice of
commentary – in other words, that the discourse of cultural
studies is akin to the classic realist novel. But that is going
too far. In the first place, as Willis argues, ethnography in
cultural studies is not reducible to naturalism: it is not just
that subjects 'speak for themselves'. Secondly, it would be
outrageous to suggest that the Marxist theory of the past
decade is reducible to social commentary. Certainly, the 'differentiated totality' traced by structuralist Marxism is a major
development from the homogeneous 'overview'. And yet the
critical point remains: that this discourse of social commentary is still reproduced, alongside Marxist analysis, and precisely it seems at those points where the 'political-intellectual
stance' is asserted.

Now these arguments do at least qualify the thesis that a
critical 'disconnection' is on the cards for cultural studies. At
the very least, we must recognise that studies of 'popular
culture' have been situated within a particular range of discur-

sive practices. There is a complex history of juxtapositions, shifts and transformations to be traced here. But also, the partial continuity between some of these practices and their nineteenth-century antecedents must cast some doubts on the claim that cultural studies involves a consistent 'critical tradition'. On the contrary, in this continuity of practices, where 'culture' is interpreted as a sign of 'crisis', it seems to me that a conventional nexus of discursive positions is reproduced. This is the 'political-intellectual stance' which Foucault has characterised as 'universal':

For a long time the 'left' intellectual spoke and was acknowledged to have the right of speaking in the capacity of master of truth and justice. He was heard, or purported to make himself heard, as the representative of the universal. To be an intellectual meant to be, a little, the consciousness/conscience of everyone. . . The intellectual is supposed to be the clear individual figure of a universality of which the proletariat is the obscure, collective form.[13]

In these terms it certainly seems appropriate to question (a) to what extent cultural studies has shifted the terrain of academic practice; and (b) if indeed current institutional developments represent a potential compromise. For Foucault of course, quite a different range of options is available. Against the 'universal' stance, he develops his concept of 'specific intellectuals': 'working. . . in specific sectors, at precise points where they are situated either by their professional conditions of work or their conditions of life (housing, the hospital, the asylum, the laboratory, the university, familial and sexual relations)'.[14] In this formulation, the process of institutionalisation is represented not as a potential threat, but as an *opportunity*. New conditions of work for teachers and researchers provide the foundation for a new kind of 'political-intellectual stance': specific struggles and alliances, rather than universalist social commentary ('the consciousness/conscience of everyone').

Today, we may well be located at a decisive moment in the history of work on popular culture. It is interesting at least to speculate on the possibilities for specific intellectual work in this field. In reading Foucault's essay, I am reminded of the passage in the *Prison Notebooks* where Gramsci spells out his prescription for the 'new intellectual':

The mode of being of the new intellectual can no longer consist in eloquence, which is an exterior and momentary mover of feelings and passions, but in active participation in practical life, as constructor, organiser, 'permanent persuader' and not just a simple orator. . . from technique-as-work one proceeds to technique-as-science and to the humanistic conception of history, without which one remains 'specialised' and does not become 'directive' (specialised and political).[15]

A translator's note makes clear that in this passage Gramsci is exploring the possibility of a *rapprochement* between the 'organic' working-class intellectual and a new politicised form of education. Are there possibilities here for cultural studies? On the one hand, certain 'organic' positions do seem possible, if extremely difficult to sustain. Here, the intellectual is no longer located in an encounter with the 'other' ('disturbance', 'surprise', etc.), but rather would articulate the demands and policies formulated by oppressed groups. Some recent feminist work can be cited in this connection;[16] and it is significant that some 'feminist ethnography' at the Centre for Contemporary Cultural Studies has precisely developed a practice of 'permanent persuasion' – working with girls, or in women's writing workshops. In this respect, working with girls presents quite a different set of political opportunities than 'working with boys'.[17]

However, the Gramsci quotation holds out another range of possibilities which may be particularly relevant at the present time. I want to draw attention to Gramsci's use of the word 'technique' in this passage, which correlates with his subsequent insistence on the importance of 'instruction' and 'discipline' in education'.[18] These kinds of words may seem quite foreign to 'progressive' practice – indeed, they may seem to belong to the pedagogical discourse of Thatcherism. But they are also, of course, quite foreign to the 'universal' practice of cultural studies: the magisterial practice of interpretation and commentary. I want to suggest that there is a space here, between Sir Keith's conception of 'training' and traditional cultural commentary, for a new kind of popular cultural practice.

For as teachers and researchers in this field, we have always privileged a particular definition of 'culture'. In the universalist discourse, 'culture' is equated with 'consciousness/conscience', i.e. with an ideological struggle over *meanings*. But in the new leisure industries, in some of the popular cultural practices analysed elsewhere in this volume (e.g. video games, home computers), *technique* (skills and practices) has the potential to displace 'meaning' as a privileged focus for development. It is what people *do* with these technologies (in terms of rules, models, calculations, etc.) that is important. The 'new intellectual' must learn to work with these practices, in the specific institutional sites where they are employed.

So I would echo Foucault in welcoming the demise of the 'universal' intellectual. For too long cultural studies has held to a nineteenth-century version of the 'political-intellectual stance' – a version which was developed, but not fundamentally shifted, by the recovery of Marxism in the seventies. In these terms, much more work can be done on the discursive history of 'popular culture', as a concept implicated in certain forms of rhetoric, narrative, and ethnographic research. But at the same time, new institutional developments (in media studies, communication studies, etc.) can be welcomed, not resisted, as providing a new focus for critical intellectual work.

Notes

1 See Stuart Hall, 'Cultural studies: two paradigms', in *Media, Culture and Society* 2, 2, 1980; Richard Johnson, 'Histories of Culture/Theories of Ideology', in Michele Barrett *et al* eds., *Ideology and Cultural Production* (London: Croom Helm, 1979); and Richard Johnson, 'Three problematics: elements of a theory of working class culture', in John Clarke *et al* eds., *Working Class Culture* (London: Hutchinson, 1979).

2 See 'Popular culture: defining our terms', U203, Block 1 Units 1/2, pp. 77-86; and 'The formation of the "cultural studies" approach', U203, Block 1 Unit 3, pp. 23-34, (Milton Keynes: Open University, 1981).

3 Louis Althusser, 'Ideology and ideological state apparatuses', in *Lenin and Philosophy*, (London: New Left Books, 1971).

4 Richard Johnson, 'What is cultural studies anyway?' (Centre for Contemporary Cultural Studies, Stencilled Occasional Paper No 74, 1983), pp. 1-10.

5 *Ibid.*, p. 6.

6 *Ibid.*, p. 9.

7 *Ibid.*, p. 5.

8 U203, Block 7 Unit 32, (Milton Keynes: © Open University, 1981).

9 It may be useful to compare Arnold's account of 'incursions':

> For a long time, as I have said, the strong feudal habits of subordination and deference continued to tell upon the working class. The modern spirit has now almost entirely dissolved those habits, and the anarchical tendency of our worship of freedom in and for itself. . . is becoming very manifest. More and more. . . this and that man, and this and that body of men, all over the country, are beginning to assert and to put in practice an Englishman's right to do what he likes; his right to march where he likes, enter where he likes, hoot as he likes, threaten as he likes, smash as he likes. All this I say, tends to anarchy. . . And one finds also that the outbreaks of rowdyism tend to become less and less of trifles, to become more frequent rather than less frequent; and that meanwhile our educated and intelligent classes remain in their majestic repose. . . *Culture and Anarchy* (Cambridge: Cambridge University Press, 1969) pp. 76-7.

The point of this comparison is not to assert definite conceptual links; rather it is to indicate a similarity of 'stance'; a rhetorical address; and in particular, the narrative of national 'crisis' which occasions the 'cultural' response.

10 Paul Willis, 'Notes on method', in Stuart Hall *et al* eds., *Culture, Media, Language*, (London: Hutchinson, 1980), p. 92.

11 The significance of Mayhew is related to his pioneering of 'qualitative' interviewing techniques, within a practice which combines 'superior journalism' with social inquiry (see Anne Humphreys, *Travels into the Poor Man's Country*, Caliban Books, 1980). Richard Johnson (1983, *op. cit.*) offers some salutary comments on this ethnographic tradition:

> We have to keep a discomforted eye on the historical pedigree and current orthodoxies of what is sometimes called 'ethnography', a practice of representing the cultures of others. The practice, like the word, already extends social distance and constructs relations of knowledge-as-power.
>
> It is important to recognise the specific origins of methods which we have adopted here and the usual problems of transformation that are involved. An adequate history of social inquiry would include the forms of philanthropic or state surveillance of working-class populations which have been a feature of the metropolitan societies at least since the eighteenth century' (p. 45)

12 The major contemporary example is Stuart Hall *et al.*, *Policing the Crisis* (London: Macmillan, 1978): 'We start with "mugging", but we end with the

way society is "policing its crisis'" (p. ix). It is not simply that a local event is totalised in narrative terms; but also that at a critical point (p. 322) the social reaction to mugging (an *ideology* of 'crisis') is taken to refer to a *real* 'crisis' in the social formation. Essentially, it is at this moment of 'realism' that cultural analysis claims the privilege of social commentary.

13 Michel Foucault, 'The political function of the intellectual', in *Radical Philosophy* 17, 1977, p. 12.

14 *Ibid.*

15 Antonio Gramsci, 'The intellectuals', in *Selections from the Prison Notebooks*, (New York: Lawrence and Wishart, 1971), p. 10.

16 I am referring in particular to socialist-feminist initiative concerning the alternative economic strategy, and the future of the labour movement, cf. Beatrix Campbell, 'Women: not what they bargained for', *Marxism Today* 26, 3, 1982; and Jean Gardiner, 'Caught in the gender trap', *Marxism Today* 28· 2, 1983.

17 Angela McRobbie and Trisha McCabe eds., *Feminism for Girls: An Adventure Story* (London: Rowtledge and Kegan Paul, 1981).

18 Antonio Gramsci, 'On education', in *op. cit.*, pp. 33ff.

Popular culture:
notes and revisions

In her chapter in this book, Tania Modleski, in as nice a way as possible, refers to my passing remark during the closing session of the seminar that there is 'an absence of feminist work around popular culture'. However much I appeal to context, to the informal nature of my remarks, or protest that that was not really what I meant, when I look at the transcript that statement does look back at me. What I actually meant then is probably no longer relevant (I think I had a vague sense that feminism had not transformed the 'popular culture debate' in the way that it had transformed other debates). What I want to say here, in this final chapter, is that, on reflection, the Popular Culture Seminar worked to dissolve many of the assumptions about popular culture which made such a routine 'mistake' possible, and the memory is of the excitement of recasting boundaries, and of thinking our way out of the security wing of the guaranteed relationship between popular culture, politics and the people which has supported so much left thinking about culture, at least in Britain, since the fifties. That relationship secured for popular culture a place within class politics, and gave the force to terms like 'cultural struggle' and 'cultural politics', but it always tended to do so by assigning to the so-called 'other social forces' a contributory rather than a transformative role. Much of the writing in this collection implicitly or explicitly questions the guarantees of that relationship.

This present chapter originated as an informal attempt to re-focus a rather wide range of issues for final discussion at the plenary session of the seminar on which this book is based. It was not intended as a magisterial summing-up, or as a respondent's response, but as an attempt to resurrect some of the difficulties of popular culture which no amount of discussion had succeeded in burying. The paper was originally billed as 'Popular culture: redefinitions', a title which now seems not only impossible but undesirable in its hubristic promise of closure. 'Notes', therefore, because that is what follows; 'revisions', more importantly, because I want to keep open an uneasy ambivalence between the excitement of re-seeing and a persistent caution towards the risks of academic revisionism.

Mass culture/popular culture

Colin MacCabe has already invoked the Oxford English Dictionary on the term 'popular': 'Of, pertaining to, or consisting of the common people. . .; constituted or carried on by the people'; 'adapted to the understanding or taste of ordinary people'; 'Finding favour with or approved by the people; liked, beloved or admired by the people, or by people generally'. The dangerous temptations of a slippage of meaning between possession, adaptation, and approval are clear. Against this set of definitions can be placed the Oxford English Dictionary's gloss of the term 'mass': '*The mass*: the generality of mankind; the main body of a race or nation', an application which begins in the seventeenth century but does not become current till the nineteenth; '*The masses*: the populace or "lower orders"', a meaning which does not become clear till the nineteenth century ('1837 Moore *Mem*. VII, 174, One of the few proofs of good Taste that "the masses", as they are called, have yet given.'); and behind these meanings, dating from *c*. 1400, is the primary definition: 'A coherent body of plastic or fusible matter (as dough, clay, metal), not yet moulded or fashioned into objects of definite shape; a lump of raw material for moulding, casting, sculpture, etc.'.

When the terms are applied to culture, the etymological distinction can be read as a convenient condensation of two distinct histories. 'Mass culture', within cultural studies, resonates not only with an etymology which associates the masses with fusible matter waiting inertly to be fashioned, but also with the pessimistic tradition of Adorno and the Frankfurt School which poses that inertia against the aggressive advances of the 'consciousness industries'. 'Popular culture', in contrast, seems to have behind it a memory of the people as agents of their own development, a memory which finds its focus in Britain in certain histories of popular resistance to the advance of capital in the nineteenth century, and which has often taken the form in cultural politics and cultural study of a Utopian desire to restore culture to the people and the people to their culture.

I am talking about echoes and memories of meaning rather than about definitions. It would clearly be absurd to suggest that the study of 'mass culture' can only be pessimistic and defensive, or that 'popular culture' can only be the property of a fully-fledged people in charge of its own destiny. Nevertheless, there does seem to be something at stake in the distinction which was not addressed by the seminar, and it is signalled in this collection by the quite striking consistency with which American contributions seem to adopt 'mass culture' as the preferred term while British contributions quite emphatically prefer 'popular culture'. It does not seem to me that in moving between the two terms we were or are addressing two distinct objects, but rather that we were speaking as the subjects of two disinct histories: national histories, to a quite large extent, both of the development of the study of culture within the academy, and also, perhaps more importantly, of the place which history and national mythology have assigned in society to 'the people' and 'the masses'. Remaining here simply at the level of the academy, in Britain, 'popular culture' is the object of a cultural studies formed in reaction to Leavis and the 'high culture' tradition. To assert popular culture as an object of academic study was, in the rhetoric of the seventies, as much a political intervention as an academic innovation, and cultural studies still bears the traces of that moment. American cultural studies traces a different descent, through distinct institutions and with different avatars and shibboleths, contesting, perhaps, empirical sociology and the pessimism of critical theory rather than the elitism of 'Eng. Lit.', threatened less by the weight of an ossified academic tradition than by the easy accommodation, the 'repressive tolerance', of the liberal arts academy. Reinforced by different myths of classes and masses, it seems inevitable that there should be national specificities within cultural studies.

I am stressing these specificities, and in the process risking extremely crude oppositions, because it seems to me that one of the most productive things which the seminar did was to place these nationally specific cultural studies into some kind of relationship, even if it is only in retrospect that we can begin to see what the relationship might lead to. From a British perspective, American cultural studies seems to work through the disciplines of the academy. We, on the other hand, not yet free from the tradition of shame which is associated in the British left with academic study, seem always to seek a very immediate engagement with a politics which cannot be found in the academy. We comfort ourselves with the slightly desperate self-assurance that while American scholarly work produces sophisticated formal and theoretical analyses, we sing all the good songs. The seminar did not put the analyses to music, but it did challenge the comforting national stereotypes, dissolve boundaries, and, most importantly, it did explore the horizon of a desire for a new cultural studies.

But, at the same time, in my insistence on retaining the

term 'popular culture' against the term 'mass culture', I do want to indicate a desire to retain memory of a popular politics.

Politics

In a paper to a History Workshop conference published in 1981 as *People's History and Socialist Theory*, Stuart Hall concludes:

> . . . just as there is no fixed content to the category of 'popular culture', so there is no fixed subject attached to it – 'the people'. 'The people' are not always back there, where they have always been, their culture untouched, their liberties and their instincts intact, still struggling on against the Norman yoke or whatever: as if, if only we can 'discover' them and bring them back on stage, they will stand up in the right, appointed place and be counted. The capacity to *constitute* classes and individuals as a popular force – that is the nature of the political and cultural struggle: to *make* the divided classes and the separated peoples – divided and separated by culture as much as by other factors – *into* a popular-democratic force.
>
> Sometimes we can be constituted as a force against the power-bloc: that is the historical opening in which it is possible to construct a culture which is genuinely popular. But, in our society, if we are not constituted like that, we will be constituted into its opposite: an effective populist force, saying 'Yes' to power. Popular culture is one of the sites where this struggle for and against a culture of the powerful is engaged. It is the arena of consent and resistance. It is partly where hegemony arises, and where it is secured. It is not a sphere where socialism – a socialist culture – already fully formed – might be simply 'expressed'. But it is one of the places where socialism might be constituted. That is why 'popular culture' matters. Otherwise, to tell you the truth, I don't give a damn about it.[1]

I find it extremely hard not to respond very positively to Stuart Hall's rhetoric: yes, popular culture matters; yes, that has to be continually reaffirmed if the study of popular culture is not to be shunted up an academic siding but is to be kept in play within the political. And yet the rhetoric also presents problems which focus the difficulties and dilemmas which many of us now have in thinking about the political and about culture. Simply, it seems quite difficult now to map the language of struggle, force and resistance on to a culture which is increasingly sophisticated and centralised in its production and dissemination, and which is increasingly experienced by the vast majority of its consumers as a comfortable and largely enjoyable necessity. Where and how is the struggle to be conducted, with whom, and with what support? Who is to construct the culture which will constitute the classes into something which at the moment they are not? These are not intended as fashionably cynical questions; nor are they provoked by a political or cultural pessimism. They are simply to call attention to a worrying disparity between the language of struggle which recalls a socialism of titanic forces and people's actual experience of contemporary culture.

The Marxist analysis of culture had to wait till the working class, on whose behalf the cultural struggle was to be conducted, were no longer active participants as a class in that stuggle. The apparatus of communications had moved on from the 'pauper press' of the nineteenth century and the left book clubs of the twentieth. This not only put into question the 'popularity' of popular culture (at least in its sense of possession), it also gives a somewhat attenuated sense of there being a struggle as anything other than a desire in the imaginary of the left intelligentsia. And yet the more 'cultural struggle' became a desire rather than a description, the more insistent it became within the language. Clearly rhetoric is a legitimate strategic instrument. The danger is, however, that the disparity between the language and the experience of socialist culture may be like that between the language of romantic fiction and the experience of romance. Seeming to refer, in both instances, to an experience that not all of us are having, the language leaves very little space between disappointed cynicism and a desperate triumphalism.

Perhaps even more seriously, the language of cultural struggle comes out of a tradition of socialism which is aggressively masculine in its historical dependence on male industrial labour. It carries the weight of masculinism into the arena of popular culture, preparing the ground for my casual 'mistake' by defining the importance of popular culture, why it matters, in a historically masculine language of force, power and struggle. The concept of cultural struggle was a strategic intervention to displace economism by asserting the effectiveness of struggles other than the struggle over the ownership of the means of production; but by polemically appropriating the language of class struggle it has placed culture within a discourse which makes it difficult to think other forms of engagement. Whatever the objects of the struggle, it is not easy to separate the history of the discourse from its assumption of a male subject.

But still, popular culture matters, and it matters for some of the very political reasons that Stuart Hall suggests: it is one of the sites where forms of consciousness and identity are constituted. In this sense it is something more than a matter for academic concern. Within the academy, always more susceptible to cynicism than to triumphalism, the dissatisfaction with where we are now, together with the very real institutional pressure to stake a claim on 'the new', produces a certain irresponsible urge to leave theoretical footsteps in the snow simply because there are no footprints there already. The academic pendulum swings along the fine line between re-seeing and revisionism: valorisation of consumption relaces insistence on production; recognition of escapism relaces the search for engagement; the centrality of contradiction makes way for the importance of identity; work makes way for relaxation and politics makes way for pleasure. Each of these shifts is important and necessary where it occurs under the pressure of a specific theoretical and political demand. The difficulty is in slowing the process which turns a radical shift into a new orthodoxy. The significance of these sea-changes within theory does not seem to me to lie in going beyond politics, but in recasting the language of the political, freeing culture from a monolithic discourse. To do that the terms need to be held, however uneasily, together, rather than one set replacing the other in a continual recantation.

In the end, what the seminar and the writings in this book seem to me to throw most seriously into question is not politics or popular culture, but the desire for the Universal Theory. The Women's Movement, national movements, ethnic and sexual movements, cannot easily be placed under the terms of a discourse which has as its unconscious the primacy of class, nor can such movements simply be subsumed within a politics which has as its imaginary the struggle of titanic forces. Yet it is precisely from the perspective of these 'peripheral' movements, rather than from the dominant 'core' of genders or nations or races secure in their historical identities, that the political urgency of popular culture can most immediately be felt. For 'peripheral' movements, culture is a practical demand, one which has to be worked out experimentally, cut to the patterns of their own desires. Reviewing Marxist positions on nationalism in the Scottish cultural journal, *Cencrastus*, Cairns Craig indicates a reason for their failure:

One of the reasons why Marxism has so signally failed to make sense of nationalism is precisely that its universalism cuts it out from the experimental basis on which nationalisms are founded: it is easy to argue the nation's role in the capitalist system; it is not easy to deny the emotions which nationalism mobilises, and one cannot discover these from the terms of the system, even if one can discover their role within it. One cannot both watch the pattern of the game and be a player in it.[2]

From the perspective of someone writing in Scotland,

then, I am as unsympathetic to the appeal to go beyond the politics of culture as I am to the promise that the national question will be answered once we have sorted out the class struggle. The terms which are appropriate to the nationalisms of developing nations may not immediately coincide with discourses of feminism or race any more than they inevitably coincide with each other: the cultural imperatives of Scotland are clearly very different from those of Nicaragua. But they are not forever autonomous, and it seems to me to be these 'peripheral' discourse which put a practical and theoretical pressure on notions of politics and culture which cannot be answered from a prescriptive universal theory, whether it be a 'classical Marxism' or a 'classical' modernism. The relationship is one of transformation, in which the terms cannot be finalised in advance. In the opposition which is posed, for example, in both Marxism and modernism, between contradiction and identity, a cultural identity takes on a different significance within a culture whose identity has always been divided or maginalised than it has within a class or a gender or a nation whose identity is secure and powerful. A national identity may be progressive at one moment and oppressive at the next. It is for this reason, rather than for the sake of an easy theoretical pluralism, that all the terms have to be kept in play, rather than one set being junked in favour of another in waves of orthodoxy. It is from the perspectives of the margins and the peripheries that popular culture is most likely to be construed not within the closure of a unifying theory, but in terms of quite concrete and particular demands and experiments.

Pleasure

Brecht talking to Benjamin in 1934:

I often imagine being interrogated by a tribunal. 'Now tell us, Mr Brecht, are you really in earnest?' I would have to admit that no,

I'm not completely in earnest. I think too much about artistic problems, you know, about what is good for the theatre, to be completely in earnest. But having said 'no' to that important question, I would add something still more important: namely, that my attitude is, *permissible*.[3]

In his introductory chapter, Colin MacCabe suggests that in relation to popular television it is crucial to discern where 'the terrain of the political is being redefined', and he identifies a central point in that reorientation as being the the 'discrimination of pleasure' and an understanding of the 'enormous machineries of desire' which are caught up in the circulation of the popular. 'It might be', he suggests, 'that what is required here is yet another return to Brecht, but this time with the focus on pleasure.' In her chapter in this book, and in her writing elsewhere,[4] Tania Modleski talks of the need to understand 'the pleasure of consumption' as a way of thinking women's involvement with popular television, a pleasure of consumption which modernism, she argues, can only associate with 'the specious good'. In a way, the two positions seem irreconcilable. Brecht, the modernist, was used in the seventies precisely to castigate the cinema of consumption and to support an insistence on a productive, active, critical relationship between spectator and text. The spectator was to be a producer of meanings, of politics; the political spectator could not simply consume; the political text was not simply about politics, but produced a political spectator. To reinsert consumption is apparently to challenge modernist critical assumptions at their foundations. I want to suggest, briefly, one of the ways in which Brecht might be reapproached as a theorist of pleasure as much as of politics, but I also want to recognise some of the particular difficulties which television holds for that reapproach.

The terms which were used to appropriate Brecht to film theory in the seventies resonate with the same discursive strategies which were used to make culture serious, a site of struggle, by associating it with industrial labour: the spectator as producer, working at the text. Time and again, Brecht had to be rescued from a puritanical anti-pleasure which was clearly a mis-reading, but was nevertheless a mis-reading already inscribed in the language. If now we are to reapproach Brecht to seek a realignment of politics and pleasure, it may be that the Brecht that we have to approach is the one who was 'not completely in earnest'.

'I even think,' said Brecht in 1922, 'that in a Shakespearean production one man in the stalls with a cigar could bring about the downfall of Western art.'[5] The man in the stalls with a cigar brings down Western art by denying it the reverence which its ceremonies demand. He (the metaphor is unfortunately both sexist and unhealthy) refuses both the self-indulgence of emotional identification and the self-denial of work, his cigar the image for Brecht of a relaxed detachment. The pleasures of what Brecht calls a 'smoker's theatre' are relaxed pleasures: pleasures which he compares to the experience of the *aficionado* at a boxing match who observes without involvement, registering the finer points and assessing the skill with which the performance is conducted.

When people in sporting establishments buy their tickets they know exactly what is going to take place; and that is exactly what does take place: viz. highly trained persons developing their peculiar powers in the way most suited to them, with the greatest sense of responsibility yet in such a way as to make one feel that they are doing it primarily for their own fun. *Against that the traditional theatre is nowadays quite lacking in character.*[6]

Clearly a considerable amount of rescue work would have to be done on Brecht's chosen metaphor, but the notion of relaxed pleasure seems to me to suggest a way of thinking about the pleasure of television, and popular culture more generally, which escapes the economic problematic of production and consumption. It seems inappropriate to expect that the theoretical and political discourse which was developed at a particular historical moment to account for the machinery of desire and identification involved in classic narrative cinema (a cinema which itself had only an imaginary coherence) would have much explanatory purchase on a television whose specific formal system owes so much to its specific conditions of viewing. Within those conditions – domestic rather than theatrical, interruptable rather than intense, controllable rather than compulsive, dispersed rather than condensed – the concept of relaxed pleasure may be more appropriate to the specifically televisual. Consumption reverses the terms and some of the 'masculine' industrial assumptions of modernism and its fetishisation of production, but it remains within the same discourse. For television, and for the conditions of contemporary popular culture, it may be more appropriate to think towards a different discourse.

But if the idea of relaxed pleasure is to be thought through politically rather than simply as a descriptive account of an audience's impassivity, Brecht still poses a difficulty to television. The difficulty hinges around the centrality which Brecht gives to the *gestus*, and to a gestural precision (again, he frequently returns to the metaphor of the boxer) which, in the theatre, continually condenses meaning in a moment of perfectly realised performance. In the first version of *What is Epic Theatre* Benjamin tells of Brecht's instructions to an actor 'to play the choosing of a wooden leg by the beggar in *Threepenny Opera* in such a way that 'just for the sake of seeing this particular turn people will plan to revisit the show at the precise moment it occurs'.[7] To which might be added Brecht's injunction in the foreword to *Antigone*: 'If the theatre is capable of showing the truth, then it must also be capable of making the sight of it a pleasure'.[8] The pleasure of Brecht's theatre is a pleasure in performance. The relaxed detachment is made political by a highly concentrated and skilled performance which does not simply show the world but which, in its condensation, makes it strange. It seems to me to be quite difficult to appropriate this to the more dispersed pleasures of television.

In his chapter, Simon Frith rightly stresses the importance of recognition as a source of pleasure on television. The point might be reinforced by recalling that during the seminar quite frequent reference was made to programmes like *Rawhide, Life with the Lyons*, and *The Grove Family*, and each seemed to have the capacity to produce in anyone over the age of thirty (within national boundaries, of course) a distinctly unacademic and affectionate response. The way in which television functions as a collectively shared experience, a popular memory, has not really been thought through. When we identify ourselves with a collective past – the fifties or 1968 – or as members of a generation, where do images come from if not from popular music or popular television? But if we are to reapproach Brecht, we would have to add, 'Recognition, yes; but recognition as if for the first time'. Without the element of distanciation, relaxed detachment, which the *gestus* intruduces – the world seen for the first time as strange rather than natural – recognition for Brecht becomes simply confirmation.

The challenge which Brecht poses, then, to the theorisation of the pleasure of television can be focused around the concept of performance. The condensation and distanciation of the *gestus* is hard to conceive within the constant dispersal of television's endless repetition. Even relative to cinema, performance seems extremely low on the list of possible pleasures of television. At the same time, that same repetition which disperses performance also creates the conditions for another central concept of Brecht's theory and theatre: the concept of 'interruption'. What the *gestus* does within the drama, like the *mie* of the Kabuki theatre which so interested Brecht, is to interrupt its flow, stopping the action in a moment of condensation, refocusing the spectator's attention. For television, it seems possible to think of the status of certain programmes – *Widows, Hill Street Blues, Boys from the Blackstuff* – in a similar way. They interrupt the flow of repetition with their difference. Recognition, yes: they are the familiar stuff of television. But as if for the first time. Both repetition *and* difference. It is perhaps programmes like these, rather than the somewhat predictable single plays of the responsible left, which suggest models for a political and pleasurable popular television.

One response to all this is to say that within the conditions of what Simon Frith describes as 'capitalist culture', in which the experience of psychic and social alienation and dissociation is becoming more and more profound, confirmation and recognition are important and necessary pleasures, and that to undervalue them is to extend the life of an inappropriate and totalistic modernism which can only find value in the dissolution of fixed identities. While I emphatically agree with this argument, I also have to own up to an unease about confirmation, and about the pleasure of consumption, which is not simply an attachment to Brecht or the heady days of the seventies, but has to do with the feeling that these concepts can only function as the terms of a defensive discourse. If there is any point at all in returning to Brecht it would seem to me to be in finding an escape from the poverty of desire which is inscribed in so much writing about television, and in developing the terms which will not simply describe television as it is, but which will also extend the parameters of desire for what it might be.

Education

Andrew Tolson, elsewhere in the book, addresses the question of popular culture and education in a very interesting way. I simply want to end here by identifying a problem in teaching popular culture in the area of its popularity. Pierre Bourdieu touches on this in his article, 'The artistocracy of culture':

. . . popular entertainment secures the spectator's participation in
the show and collective participation in a festivity. . .This is the
very opposite of the detachment of the aesthete, who, as is seen
when he appropriates one of the objects of popular taste (e.g.
Westerns or strip-cartoons), introduced a distance, a gap – the
measure of his distant distinction – vis-à-vis 'first-degree' perception, by displacing the interest from the 'content', characters, plot,
etc., to the form, to the specifically artistic effects which are only
appreciated *relationally*, through a comparison with other works,
which is incompatible with immersion in the singularity of the
work immediately given.[9]

Teaching popular culture is like 'teaching pleasure': how do
you 'teach pleasure'? How do you examine it? How do you
grasp pleasure or popularity without passing them through
some distancing mechanism of form, history, context, which
separates them from their pleasure and their popularity? Even
to identify popular culture is to lift it out of its area of popularity; to teach it is always to risk reconstituting it as something other than popular (a point which students are quick
to point out when we try to pass off a forties Hollywood
movie as a 'popular' film).

It is a necessary problem, but it seems to me to be one
that we should be quite sensitive to. It could be avoided if
we were content to teach the 'appreciation' of popular culture
(to reveal it, that is, as something which has to be taken
seriously) or to demystify it. But if we are also going to consider popular culture as something active and present, it
seems to me that we have to be able to identify our own
participation in its popularity and pleasure, and erode the
sense – the measure in our writing and our teaching of our
'distant distinction' – that popular culture is what *other*
people like.

Footnote

As a matter of fact, at times I have even caught myself viewing the word 'culture' with suspicion. It seemed to have an un-American look to me, sort of snobbish and affected, as if it thought it was better than the next fellow. Actually, as I understand it, culture isn't that kind of snooty word at all. As I see it, a person's culture represents his appraisal of the things that make up life. And a fellow becomes cultured, I believe, by selecting that which is fine and beautiful in life and throwing aside that which is mediocre and phoney.[10]

Not Leavis, not Arnold: Walt Disney.

Notes

1 Stuart Hall, 'Notes on deconstructing "the popular"', in *People's History and Socialist Theory*, ed. R. Samuel (London: Routledge and Kegan Paul (History Workshop Series), 1981), p. 239.

2 Cairns Craig, 'Nation and history', *Cencrastus* 19, winter 1984, p. 15.

3 'Conversations with Brecht', in Walter Benjamin, *Understanding Brecht* (London: New Left Books, 1973), pp. 106-7.

4 Tania Modleski, *Loving with a Vengeance* (London: Methuen, 1982).

5 John Willett ed., *Brecht on Theatre* (London: Methuen, 1974), p. 8.

6 *Ibid.*, p. 6.

7 Quoted in Walter Benjamin, 'What is epic theatre? (first version)', in *Understanding Brecht, op. cit.*, p. 6.

8 *Brecht on Theatre, op. cit.*, p. 209.

9 Pierre Bourdieu, 'Aristocracy of culture', *Media, Culture and Society* 2, 2, 1980, p. 239.

10 Quoted in Russell Davies, 'Dreams are always in bad taste', *The Listener*, 16 February 1984.